Apparel Production Management
and the Technical Package

Apparel Production Management
and the Technical Package

Paula J. Myers-McDevitt

FAIRCHILD BOOKS NEW YORK

Vice President & General Manager,
Education & Conference Division: Elizabeth Tighe

Executive Editor: Olga T. Kontzias

Senior Associate Acquiring Editor: Jaclyn Bergeron

Assistant Acquisitions Editor: Amanda Breccia

Editorial Development Director: Jennifer Crane

Associate Development Editor: Lisa Vecchione

Creative Director: Carolyn Eckert

Production Director: Ginger Hillman

Production Editor: Jessica Rozler

Copyeditor: Joanne Slike

Ancillaries Editor: Noah Schwartzberg

Cover Design: Andrea Lau

Front Cover Art: Courtesy of iStock Photo

Back Cover Art: © foodfolio/Alamy

Text Design: Tronvig Group

Page Composition: Tom Helleberg

Director, Sales & Marketing: Brian Normoyle

Library of Congress Catalog Card Number:
2009934621
ISBN: 978-1-56367-869-1
GST R 133004424
Printed in the United States of Americs
TP09

Contents

Extended Contents

Preface

With increased globalization of garment production and the need to unify product information, *Apparel Production Management and the Technical Package* is essential for fashion students and professionals who wish to understand this exploding trend in production management and gain the skills necessary for this new universe of apparel manufacturing. The text provides an overview of production management in the global marketplace while examining in detail the components of the technical package, or tech-pack, a series of forms that define a garment's specifications and that is critical to ensuring that a particular style is executed correctly and in the most cost- and time-efficient manner possible. The text is laid out simply:

- Parts I and II provide information on production management, costing, planning and scheduling, and global production, including sourcing, assembly and finishing, and packaging and distribution (Chapters 1 to 6).
- Part III is organized as a production workbook. This section contains an overview of the technical package (Chapter 7) and features its seven major components, with descriptions, instructions, and examples for each (Chapters 8 to 14).
- Also included throughout the text are Industry Insider profiles, readings about real professionals within the industry—their strengths, their talents, their strategies for success, and their business philosophy.
- The appendices contain important resources, including basic flat-sketch and body form croquis, basic industrial sewing stitches, a button selector gauge, care labeling regulations, and basic measurement points. Also included is Appendix F, which contains duplicates of the tech-pack templates from the laboratory applications at the end of Chapters 8 through 14. This allows students to use the templates for their assignments. In this appendix, you will find the following: design sheet, illustration sheet, fabric sheet, component sheet, label/packaging sheet, detail/construction sheet, and spec sheet.

USING THIS TEXT

Who in the production team is given the task of assembling the production package varies by company. Ultimately, however, the production manager is responsible for ensuring the accuracy of the technical package. Companies vary their technical packages based on the needs of the company; however, most companies include the seven components highlighted in this text. As you work through the chapters in Part III, you will be given the opportunity to create your own technical package, using either a garment of your own design or one provided by your instructor. Not everyone will have the skills needed to complete every sheet in the workbook. Do not be discouraged. In the industry the production manager must collaborate with the merchandising, design, technical, and sales departments to obtain all the information contained within a technical package. The author of this text has worked in production management, technical design, and quality assurance (Box P.1).

BOX P.1 Industry Insider Paula J. Myers-McDevitt

This textbook is Paula Myers-McDevitt's second with Fairchild Books. Her first, in its second edition, is *Complete Guide to Size Specification and Technical Design*. In addition to writing, Paula has taught post-secondary school and worked in the fashion industry.

Myers-McDevitt's career started in production management, as a lingerie assistant. After a few years of inventory control, patternmaking management, and costing, she moved to what was then the newly developing field of technical design. She worked for large merchandising houses such as May Merchandising Group, Federated Department Stores, and Conston Corporation. As a technical design manager, Paula was able to travel nationally and internationally for business. Her last full-time job in the industry was for a children's wear company based in the Philadelphia suburbs, running the quality assurance department.

In the late 1990s Myers-McDevitt started working part time as an instructor at Harcum College, teaching courses in merchandising, advertising, and business. She moved on to Cheyney University of Pennsylvania's Design and Merchandising Department, again teaching a variety of classes. It was during this time that she wrote her first text. Myers-McDevitt has also taught at Immaculata University; all three institutions are in the Philadelphia suburbs where she now resides.

It has been her pleasure to research and write this latest text, on production management and the technical package, using her more than 20 years of industry and postsecondary education experience.

Acknowledgments

Once again, I would like to thank the wonderful staff at Fairchild Books, who have made this process so seamless: Elizabeth Tighe, Olga Kontzias, Jaclyn Bergeron, Amanda Breccia, Jennifer Crane, Lisa Vecchione, Carolyn Eckert, Avital Aronowitz, Andrea Lau, and Jessica Rozler. Your support and expertise are invaluable.

Thank you to the following educators who reviewed my proposal and offered many helpful suggestions and improvements: Mary Androsiuk, Kwantlen University; Jennifer L. Clevenger, Virginia Tech; Cynthia L. Istook, North Carolina State University; Jeanie Lisenby, Miami International University of Art and Design; Natalie Nixon, Philadelphia University; Eulanda A. Sanders, Colorado State University; and Shari Schopp, the Art Institute of California—San Francisco.

I am also indebted to several industry professionals who sent me technical packages and who also took the time to send me profiles or let me interview them. Thank you Zoë Anderson, ZLA Design; Kiyomi Chansamone, TechPackCentral; Teri Davis, Confluence Design; Heather and Geoffrey Krasnov, Style Source Inc.; Jillian Krebsbach, Macy's Merchandising Group; Patrice Robson, Patrice Robson Design; Rubina, Just D-zine; and Jennifer Stady, Ed Hepp, and Emily Bulfin, Laundry Studio.

Finally, big thank-yous go to my husband, Chris, and to my son, Andrew. They have supported me through the writing of another text with their computer expertise, their endless copy and mail services, and, more important, their compassion and love.

Apparel Production Management
and the Technical Package

Introduction to Production Management

PART ONE

Production Management

THE PRODUCTION DEPARTMENT

Production is the functional department of any apparel company. The **production department** is responsible for making sure that raw goods are procured and made into finished goods. Learning the workings of the production department is critical to understanding the value of the technical package, which you will learn about in Part III of this text.

In production, a good administrator carefully coordinates all aspects of the production process, from execution to delivery. Such precision makes the department very technical and detail-oriented. As a result, the production department is a cost source, not a money-making source; in other words, the production department does not directly generate revenue for the company.

PRODUCTION WORK IS:

- administrative
- detail-oriented
- technical

A sharp production team is key. The role of the production team **is to**

- coordinate fabric and trim deliveries to the factories
- schedule raw materials for construction
- schedule and track production
- ship finished goods to retailers

Production employees must know all operations, including sewing and packaging, care labeling laws, import and customs laws (when working oversees), and quality assurance and control systems. Knowing these functions of production is imperative when sending work to the factories.

Controlling the flow of work is an important aspect of production as well. The team must make sure there is enough work scheduled to keep the factories running, yet not so much that they need to bill for costly overtime. Moreover, in order for every element of production to fall into place, the team must handle with expertise and exact timing their various tasks, whether assessing contractors, purchasing garment components, or training personnel.

OBJECTIVES

- Understand the organizational structure of a standard production department.

- Understand the basic job skills and requirements of each position within the production department.

- Cite challenges in production management.

Because precision and coordination are essential to the success of a production department, a competent **production manager** must lead the team. One of the tools the production manager uses to ensure smooth execution is the technical package, also known as the tech–pack. Employees at the source (each step of the process) produce the components of the technical package; however, it is ultimately the production manager's job to coordinate the processes that go into the making of the finished package.

In some companies, top management, such as Gucci's chief operating officer, Patrizio di Marco, maintains a close relationship with the production staff as well (Box 1.1).

The following departments help develop the technical package:

- Design
- Patternmaking
- Technical design/size specification
- Quality assurance
- Sales

The technical package is sent, along with the cutting ticket or purchase orders, to suppliers, manufacturers, finishers, and distributors. Users with direct links—access to a company server with fashion industry software (Gerber Technology, Lectra, and Apparel Information Management Systems [AIMS] are among the top)—can access this information immediately.

BOX 1.1 Industry Insider Patrizio di Marco

The chief executive officer of the $3.2 billion Gucci empire believes the best way to run a business is to get to know its people—especially the production staff. "I hate it when you only talk to those directly reporting to you—you don't create a team," says the personable Patrizio di Marco (Zargani and Conti 2009). Quality Italian craftsmanship is one of Gucci's great assets.

The Gucci CEO Mark Lee announced in September 2008 that he would be leaving, opening the door for di Marco, who had spearheaded a turnaround at Bottega Veneta. He is con-

sidered a great optimist in the world of luxury goods for his insistence on returning the Bottega brand to its former days of understated elegance and for looking forward to the challenge at Gucci. To di Marco, "Vision is first and foremost about the ability to see with absolute clarity where you want to go . . . being brave and sticking to your long term view. And go, if necessary, without ever compromising your integrity, against the prevailing trends in the market, no matter how difficult the environment is" (Lipke 2008).

THE PRODUCTION TEAM

As you can see, the production department is in charge of getting the line produced and making goods available for consumption. Let us take a closer look at this team and how its members relate to one another (Figure 1.1, next page).

Production manager—The person in charge of the production team. The production manager is responsible for setting and meeting production deadlines. Production managers make sure that work is carried out smoothly and supervise procedures for efficiency. They must be organized and computer-literate and have an affinity for detail. A production manager may also have a business administration, management, engineering, or apparel management degree. Many production managers have worked their way up through the ranks by starting as a production assistant or in a similar position.

Production assistant—An entry-level or lower management position; this person reports to the production manager. The production assistant must have good oral and written communication skills and be computer-literate and attentive to detail. Duties may include confirming quantities, styles, colors, and delivery dates; tracking fabrics and trims; maintaining cost sheets; tracking production of the salespersons' samples and swatch cards; coordinating lab dips; and monitoring deliveries.

Inventory management clerk—The person responsible for tracking and maintaining records on all merchandise owned by the merchandise wholesaler/manufacturer at any given time. The inventory clerk must be detail-oriented and computer-literate and have good math skills. This position is occasionally part of the production assistant's job, depending on the size of the company.

Scheduling clerk/manager—This person does the production scheduling in the manufacturing (sewing) plant. The scheduling manager works closely with senior management and sales in order to schedule production according to projected sales. The scheduling manager must make sure that all garment components are received and that delivery dates are met. This person must be able to foresee and solve potential production problems. Computer skills and attention to detail are crucial.

Purchasing agent—This person is in charge of purchasing fabrics and other garment components. Purchasing agents work closely with the design team, obtaining pertinent fabric and component information. Depending on their level, purchasing agents may write purchase orders and be called upon to negotiate price points with suppliers. Computer and math skills, plus attention to detail, are imperative in this position.

PRODUCTION DEPARTMENT DIVISION OF LABOR

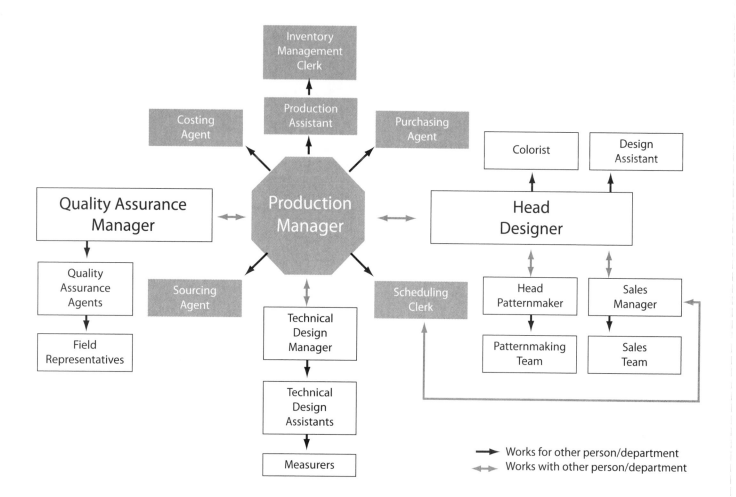

Figure 1.1

Production department division of labor. The chart maps the relationships between production team members in a typical fashion production department.

Sourcing agent—The person who locates factories for production. The sourcing agent knows the factories' capabilities and can recommend the best fit for a particular style. Sourcing agents may work on production price quotes and uncover design or assembly issues. Knowledge of import laws and limitations is required, as is foreign and domestic travel; therefore, this person must be well-groomed and have an understanding of foreign customs. The sourcing agent will need to rely on experience and intuition when choosing a factory to produce his or her company's goods. Good oral and written communication skills are needed.

Costing agent—A person who pulls together the elements of a garment (material/fabric, trims and other components, plus labor and shipping) to achieve workable costs. Good math skills are key. Experience, training, intuition, and negotiating skills will help the costing agent find a price that is right for the buyer yet profitable for the company.

Quality control/assurance agent—This can be performed by one person or by a separate department working with the production team. The basic role of quality control is to ensure that every garment produced meets the standards of the company. This position requires experience and technical training. The quality control agent must know every component of a garment, from fiber and fabric, to design, to patternmaking, to construction, to labeling, to performance. The agent will have apprenticed for several years and may have an engineering or other Bachelor of Science degree. Attention to detail is important.

CHALLENGES IN PRODUCTION

A production manager encounters many difficulties daily on the job. However, there are two major challenges facing today's production manager and staff:

1. *Tighter costing*
A result of increased competition, this is one of the foremost challenges. Price points are very important to today's consumers.

Expensive material and labor components—These are forcing many U.S. manufactures to conduct business overseas, where these costs are typically cents on the dollar (Figure 1.2).

2. *The Quick Response system*
A shortening of the cycling time of the production and distribution chain is the third challenge for today's production staff. Although a successful Quick Response (QR) strategy can save a company money through reduced inventory and increased turnover, it can shorten the planning time or lead time, or both, in the production process.

Figure 1.2
As production managers move manufacturing overseas, they are finding competition stiff; the number of exhibitors at the 2009 Material World Miami trade show fell to 268, compared with 400 during 2008's edition. *Source: Photo courtesy of* Women's Wear Daily.

Because of these challenges, production personnel are always looking for and sourcing new production plants. It takes time and energy to find and test new plants. Manufacturers are constantly looking for ways to save money, increase production, and shorten turnaround; it is the job of the production manager and staff to find those solutions.

Box 1.2 profiles Pepe and Reyes Amat, a husband and wife who confront the challenges of running and designing for, respectively, a longstanding family business.

PRODUCTION MANAGEMENT LAB
Laboratory Applications

1. Aisha is a recent college graduate with a BS degree in Fashion and Clothing Technology who just landed a job as a production assistant for an apparel manufacturer.

    a. What would her responsibilities as production assistant include? Is travel required of Aisha as an assistant production manager? Please support your answer.

    b. What skills could Aisha develop to further her career in production?

    c. What training might she need to prepare her for becoming a production manager?

2. Two years ago, after design school, Dominique and Patrice started a small swimwear company based in Florida. They have several local seamstresses who "sew" their line for production. To grow, however, they need to contract with a manufacturer. A friend owns a plant in the Florida area, or they can look for a jobber overseas. What do you recommend for Dominique and Patrice, and why?

3. Choose a position in production other than production manager. Research this position, and write a short paper (two to three pages) about its duties and challenges.

BOX 1.2   Industry Insiders Pepe and Reyes Amat

The Spanish footwear maker Pepe Amat and his family have been making shoes for more than 80 years in Elda, Spain. The products are sold under the label Magrit, which was shortened from the company's original name, Margarita. The family also make shoes for famous brands, including Carolina Herrera and Jil Sander. Reyes Amat, Pepe's wife, designs shoes for the family business.

In "Designer Digest: Husband-and-Wife Teams", Amat discusses the philosophy behind the line, saying it is one in which "the designers create with a 'total freedom of thought.'" For Pepe, "influences such as the environment and their way of life also figure into the mix, resulting in luxurious shoes that make women feel like 'objects of desire'" (Gollin 2009).

As for the challenges of working together, Pepe believes that his main task is to manage the design team ("It is not only Reyes and me") (Gollin 2009). He feels that although each has a separate job to accomplish, both he and Reyes are united in their mission to create quality shoes.

TABLE 1.1   **Duties, Strengths, and Skills of the Production Team**

Production Manager

- Executes the sourcing strategy for a category of merchandise.
- Assesses vendors, factories, mill capabilities, and capacities against line plans.
- Plans for volume, quota, target prices, and lead time.
- Financially accountable for sales and profit margin.
- Originates and executes calendar and production schedule.
- Is responsible for precost estimate and final negotiations.
- Places orders and communicates with vendor; maintains realistic expectations of sourcing.
- Represents production team; represents manufacturing in fit process.

Production Assistant

- Executes all production steps, from original sample development to bulk delivery.
- Owns purchase order entry process.
- Monitors and tracks styles through production to arrival in distribution center.
- Communicates all import-related information to import manager.
- Orders tickets, hangtags, and other marketing needs.

Quality Assurance Manager

- Works with vendors and factories to identify and resolve all manufacturing problems.
- Develops and evaluates factory technical and production teams.
- Sources factories, evaluates vendor compliance.
- Travels.
- Inspects work in progress at factories, resolves issues on-site, final inspection.
- Partners with technical services to ensure consistent standards.

Strength and Skills

- Computer-literate.
- Communicate in a direct, clear, and persuasive manner.
- Organized; able to prioritize workflow.
- Have management skills.
- Proactive; seeks new ideas, products, and processes.
- Able to work on a team.
- Have a specialized technical expertise.
- Have an entrepreneurial spirit.
- Understand your customer and their relationship with your brand.

Adapted from http://mycareer.com

REFERENCES

Gollin, Randi. "Designer Digest: Husband-and-Wife Teams." *WWD*, February 9, 2009. http://www.wwd.com/footwear-news/romance-language-1973408.

Harder, Frances. *Fashion for Profit: A Professional's Complete Guide to Designing, Manufacturing, and Marketing a Successful Line.* 8th ed. Rolling Hills Estates, CA: Fashion Business Incorporated, 2008.

Lipke, David. "Go Your Own Way." *WWDRetail,* November 12, 2008. http://www.wwd.com/retail-news/go-your-own-way-1856080#/article/retail/news/go-your-own-way-1856080?full=true.

MyCareer.com. http://www.mycareer.com/search.php (accessed August 21, 2008).

Myers-McDevitt, Paula J. *Complete Guide to Size Specification and Technical Design.* New York: Fairchild Publications, 2004.

Zargani, Luisa, with contributions from Samantha Conti. "Di Marco Takes Hands-on Approach at Gucci." *WWD*, April 1, 2009. http://www.wwd.com/markets-news/di-marco-takes-hands-on-approach-at-gucci-2088389.

Costing

2

THE COST–PROFIT RELATIONSHIP

The relationship between cost and profit is a fundamental theory of business management. **Cost** is the outlay of expenditure, or dollar amount, the company has invested in a product. **Profit** is the surplus remaining after total costs are deducted from total returns.

For a company to make a profit, revenue—the gross income, or total sales, of the company's product during a specific period of time—must exceed cost. Consequently, a company needs to generate revenue consistently and successfully in order to survive.

EXPENDITURES INCLUDE:

- cost of materials
- physical plant (place of business)
- employee benefits
- taxes
- insurance
- miscellaneous expenses

When costs exceed revenues, a loss is incurred. Therefore, business managers must pay very close attention to all overhead in order to keep ahead of rising costs. In addition, price—the dollar value asked for and received in exchanged for a product—is very important. If a price is set too high, consumers will not buy the product, and an exchange will not take place, leaving the company with a great deal of overhead, and there will not be a profit. If the price is set too low, the exchange takes place, but expenditures are not met, and again there will not be a profit. A perfect (medium) price must be set to ensure success; this is called costing.

THE STAGES OF COSTING

Costing a garment is the monetary value invested or used to produce a garment. However, achieving a garment cost is more complex than one might think. There are actually four stages of costing a garment may go through to reach its final cost. In putting together a cost plan, a manufacturer may utilize anywhere from one to

- Understand the cost–profit relationship.

- List the four stages of costing.

- Understand the differences between direct, absorption, and activity-based costing methods.

- Explain the breakdown of product costs on a cost sheet.

all four of the steps, depending on the company's size and structure. Some companies hire cost consultants to help with the process; TechPackCentral is one such firm. Box 2.1 profiles two other consultants, Don Eugene and Bennett Gross, of Callydus.

The four stages of costing are as follows:

1. *Preliminary costing*

Preliminary costing is done before samples are made, during the product development stage (also known as the preadoption phase) of the process. During this stage, estimates are made based on the costs of similar styles that have been already been produced. New labor and fabric estimates are added to create a more accurate estimate and thus make certain a design will not be too costly to produce. This can save valuable time and resources not only for the design staff but for the production and merchandising teams as well.

2. *Cost estimating*

Cost estimating occurs after samples have been made and just prior to line adoption. To determine this estimate, the costing agent uses a cost sheet, listing each garment component, from fabrics (also known as piece goods), to trim, to findings. Labor, manufacturing, and administration costs; sales expenses; and expected profits must also be added to the cost sheet. Because it is based on the sample and sample yardage, this estimate offers the company a relative price point against which it can measure expenditures. For this reason, this estimate is sometimes called the budget cost.

BOX 2.1   **Industry Insiders Don Eugene and Bennett Gross**

Don Eugene and Bennett Gross are good at saving money. That is what they, and their partners at Callydus, do for their clients (law firms, retail and manufacturing companies, publishers, and others), saving them a combined $135 million in Callydus's first 2 years of business.

Eugene and Gross spend up to 2 weeks assessing how clients can reduce spending and then set up a cost plan. Gross says, "'Think of it like running a household. You have to be cost-conscious, but you have other priorities . . . . You don't necessarily have time to check the fuel bill to see if you're getting the best rate, or looking at something like biofuel. We do things [others] can't do'" (Moin 2008).

Gross is one of the founding members of Callydus, with more than 25 years of business and legal experience. He began his career at the management firm Weil, Gotshal and Manges; he later went on to become a group vice president at R. H. Macy and Company, a senior vice president at Caldor Corporation, and a managing director at Huron Consulting Group. He received a JD from Georgetown University Law Center and a BA in Philosophy from Pennsylvania State University.

Eugene was formally the president of I. Magnin and Company as well as a senior executive at R. H. Macy and Company. In addition, he has provided financial and operational advice to an array of businesses and government agencies and commissions. Don was appointed by President Ronald Reagan to the Grace Commission as a member of a task force assigned to reduce expenses at the Department of Defense, the Defense Logistics Agency, and the General Services Administration.

3. *Detailed costing*

Detailed, or production, costing is done after the styles have been adopted into the line but before production. Costing at this stage is more accurate, because it is based on production markers rather than sample yardage. Anything that might have been overlooked in the cost estimating stage can and will be picked up here; this is the time for rolling up loose ends (hence the term *roll-up costs*). Actual production costs based on specific sewing methods are also available at this stage. As a result, the design will often be modified to make the garment more affordable in mass production; for example, the sweep of a full skirt might be reduced a few inches, or a pant with self-fabric pockets might be changed to one with lining fabric pockets instead.

4. *Actual costs*

Actual costs are determined after production. This is one of the most important costing processes. The cost accountant or chief financial officer (CFO) within the company will be most interested in learning the actual costs of production. These costs are determined by collecting all of the data from production—the actual cost of materials, piece goods, trims, findings, labor, manufacturing, and so on. Occasionally, even with the best costing safeguards behind it, garments costs spiral out of control for unforeseen reasons, and budgeted costs are exceeded. When this happens, the company must take a loss for garments that have already been produced. It must then successfully reengineer the garment design, or the production process, for future production, or else the style that was too expensive will have to be dropped from the line.

Managers uses the preliminary costs outlined above during the manufacturing process to determine if a designer's concept is

- feasible
- producible
- commercial
- marketable
- profitable

Actual costs are also used by the company to

- justify the purchase of new equipment
- hire new employees
- expand offices
- expand production facilities

Once a company has gone through its stages of costing, it must track all expenses and income, coming in and going out. The methods that are used to achieve this goal are called **costing methods**.

COSTING METHODS

Quarterly and annual profit-and-loss reports are used to track all expenses (costs) and income. *Cost accounting* is the term used for establishing the budget and determining the actual cost of the company's operations and expenses. Managers use cost accounting to support their decisions for cutting costs and improving profits. Managers rely on three common costing methods to calculate the cost of running a business:

1. *Variable costing*

Variable costing (also known as direct costing or marginal costing) is an account analysis method that uses only costs of production that vary with output of units as product costs. Nonvariable direct materials, direct labor, and variable manufacturing overhead costs are included in product costs under variable costing. Fixed manufacturing overhead is not treated as a product cost under this method but rather as a period cost, meaning it is charged off against revenue each period.

Let us take a look at a direct cost sheet sample. Note that all the material, trims and findings, and labor costs are on the sheet; what is not on the sheet are any of the overhead costs. These have been included in the markup and will be charged against revenue (Figure 2.1).

2. *Absorption costing*

Absorption, or full, costing is an engineering approach to costing that uses all costs of production as product costs, regardless of whether they are variable or fixed in nature. In the absorption costing method, a portion of fixed manufacturing overhead is allocated to each unit of product until sold. This method can be risky, as direct labor costs and overhead may not be accurate; they are an applied rate, which is arbitrary. Looking at the cost sheet provided (Figure 2.2), you will see that all costs, including materials, trims and findings, labor, and overhead are included. The danger with this method is that although some costs, like fabrics, trims, and labor, will be fixed, overhead costs may vary and thus not reflect a true rate. The markup for absorption costing is less than with variable costing because of the addition of overhead costs.

3. *Activity-based costing*

Activity-based costing (ABC) is a high and low approach to costing that enables managers to cost out components to business specifications and process improvements. ABC uses a cost system built on direct labor and overhead costs by determining the demand on resources. ABC is a great diagnostic tool for focusing on overhead and reducing labor, but it often misses fabric and component costs, which in fashion can add up to 50 percent of the cost sheet. The ABC cost sheet (Figure 2.3) shows the costs for labor and overhead. This sheet does not usually

DIRECT COST SHEET

Date: 8-12-09				Style #58620
Description: Men's two-piece suit				Season: Stock year-round
				Selling price: $225.00 retail
Size range: 34–48	Colors: Stock Blue and Stock Gray			
Marker yardage: 39.6	Allowance			

1. MATERIAL	YARDS	PRICE	AMOUNT	
Forman 104″	39.6	3.65	$144.54	
	0	0.00	$0.00	
Lining	21.25	1.57	$33.36	
Interfacing	2.33	0.23	$0.54	
TOTAL MATERIAL COST			**$178.44**	

2. TRIMS AND FINDINGS	QUANT.	PRICE	AMOUNT	
Buttons	132	0.45	$59.40	
Pads	24	0.72	$17.28	
Zippers	24	0.72	$17.28	
Thread	12	0.42	$5.04	
Labels and handtags	12	0.05	$0.60	
Outside Services	0	0.00	$0.00	
	0	0.00	$0.00	
	0	0.00	$0.00	
TOTAL TRIMMINGS COST			**$99.60**	

3. LABOR				
Cutting	12.00	0.30	$3.60	
Sewing	12.00	3.25	$39.00	
Finishing	12.00	0.40	$4.80	
Grading	12.00	0.30	$3.60	
Marking	12.00	0.30	$3.60	
	0	0.00	$0.00	
TOTAL LABOR COST			**$54.60**	

4. TOTAL COST		$332.64
5. MARKUP	75%	
6. WHOLESALE PRICE		$1330.55
Suggested retail:	50%	$2661.11

Figure 2.1 Sample direct cost sheet.

ABSORPTION COST SHEET					
Date: 8-12-09				Style #58620	
Description: Men's two-piece suit				Season: Stock year-round	
				Selling price: $225.00 retail	
Size range: 34–48		Colors: Stock Blue and Stock Gray			
Marker yardage: 39.6			Allowance		
1. MATERIAL	YARDS	PRICE	AMOUNT		
Forman 104"	39.6	3.65	$144.54		
Lining	21.25	1.57	$33.36		
Interfacing	2.33	0.23	$0.54		
TOTAL MATERIAL COST				$178.44	
2. TRIMS AND FINDINGS	QUANT.	PRICE	AMOUNT		
Buttons	132	0.45	$59.40		
Pads	24	0.72	$17.28		
Zippers	24	0.72	$17.28		
Thread	12	0.42	$5.04		
Labels and handtags	12	0.05	$0.60		
TOTAL TRIMMINGS COST				$99.60	
3. LABOR					
Cutting	12.00	0.30	$3.60		
Sewing	12.00	3.25	$39.00		
Finishing	12.00	0.40	$4.80		
Grading	12.00	0.30	$3.60		
Marking	12.00	0.30	$3.60		
TOTAL LABOR COST				$54.60	
4. OTHER EXPENDITURES					
Salaries—administrative		83.16	$83.16		(Pretotal costs x 25%)
Mortgage and utilities		24.95	$24.95		(Pretotal costs x 7.5%)
Shipping labor and overhead		16.63	$16.63		(Pretotal costs x 5%)
Sales—general expenses		33.26	$33.26		(Pretotal costs x 10%)
Allowance—seconds and returns		33.26	$33.26		(Pretotal costs x 10%)
TOTAL EXPENDITURES				$191.26	
5. TOTAL COST				$523.90	
6. MARKUP	60%				
7. WHOLESALE PRICE				$1309.75	
Suggested retail:	50%			$2619.50	

Figure 2.2 Sample absorption cost sheet.

ACTIVITY-BASED COST SHEET

Date: 8-12-09				Style #58620
Description: Men's two-piece suit				Season: Stock year-round
				Selling price: $225.00 retail

Size range: 34–48	Colors: Stock Blue and Stock Gray		
Marker yardage: 39.6	Allowance		

1. LABOR

		Allowance	
Cutting	12.00	0.30	$3.60
Sewing	12.00	3.25	$39.00
Finishing	12.00	0.40	$4.80
Grading	12.00	0.30	$3.60
Marking	12.00	0.30	$3.60
TOTAL LABOR COST			**$54.60**

2. OTHER EXPENDITURES

Salaries—administrative		83.16	$83.16
Mortgage and utilities		24.95	$24.95
Shipping labor and overhead		16.63	$16.63
Sales—general expenses		33.26	$33.26
Allowance—seconds and returns		33.26	$33.26
TOTAL EXPENDITURES			**$191.26**

3. SUBTOTAL COST	$254.96
4. ESTIMATED MATERIAL COSTS	$278.04
5. TOTAL COSTS	$533.00
6. MARKUP 60%	
7. WHOLESALE PRICE	$1332.50
Suggested retail: 50%	$2619.50

On a industry ABC sheet the production manager would use an average of high and low costs from old and new styles to derive these figures. The figures from the direct and absorption cost sheet have been used simply for illustrative purposes.

An industry ABC sheet would also stop at the subtotal cost. The material costs have been included in order to compare this sheet with others, if used for production purposes.

Figure 2.3 Sample activity-based cost sheet.

include materials; they are included here for illustrative purposes. This sheet would not normally be used for costing a garment, but rather for focusing on overhead costs and expansion, such as justifying new equipment or added personnel.

BREAKING DOWN PRODUCT COST

Beyond business expenses and labor, designers have a major role in deciding the cost of the product, because they specify the initial materials. Sometimes a garment

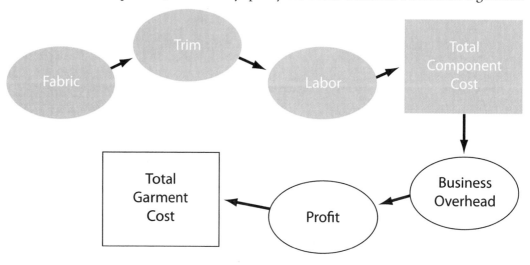

Figure 2.4

Component costs, plus overhead and profit, equal total garment cost.

will not be saleable because it has been overdesigned or because the materials are simply too costly; therefore, it is imperative that each garment be costed before production to make sure it is producible. To determine **product cost**—the sum of all costs associated with the production of a specific quantity of goods—those costs must be broken down into specific components.

The components of material costs (Figure 2.4) are

- piece goods
- trims and findings

Costing is done before production, and planning can begin to ensure the garment can be manufactured and sold at an affordable price. Sample garments for production are generally a size 8 in the showroom. However, the piece goods marker (Figure 2.5) must reflect both large and small sizes. It must therefore be weighted in a manner that is consistent with the manufacturer's consumer image. For example, if the customer base from size 6 to 16 was generally small, the marker could be cut 2, 3, 2, 2, 1, 1, 1; however, if the customer base was a more average size, then the marker might be cut a more traditional 1, 2, 3, 3, 3, 2, 1. These ranges, representing the sizes designated by retail orders or projections, per dozen, will affect the total marker yardage and thus the fabric costs.

Fabrics known as piece goods (fabrics made and sold in standard widths and lengths) are generally the largest cost of a garment and so are often listed first on the cost sheet. They are generally measured in yards, unless knitted. Trims are usually listed next. Trims are measured in yards or yards per roll. Findings (buttons, snaps, and so on) are next; they are sold by the gross (144 per package). Interfacings, zippers, and threads all must be counted and listed on the cost sheet. Labels, hangtags, tickets, Dennison bars, hangers, and polybags are additional costs that should also be added, although some manufacturers prefer to count these as expenditures.

Labor costs, also expensive, can be difficult to break down if a manufacturer is using a jobber (an independent factory), because the jobber may not be willing to disclose its sequential list of operations and pricing—that is, its method of sequencing production. It is common in the industry for manufacturers (and retailers) to use offshore factories that will not provide a detailed costing list. This list is not necessary, as long as the total labor price is provided on the cost sheet (Figure 2.6).

In this example, from TechPackCentral, a camisole has been costed out for a client (Figure 2.7).

Figure 2.5

Inside the Max Mara factory in Reggio Emilia, Italy, a marker reflecting several sizes is spread and cut. *Source: Photo by Dave Yoder, courtesy of* Women's Wear Daily.

Figure 2.6

In Fashionshare, each
SKU has its own page,
with information
about costing and
order status.
Source: Courtesy of
Women's Wear Daily.

Figure 2.7

Sample cost sheet from
TechPackCentral.

Juniors				KC798					Spring 2007
				Camisole					

Cost Sheet	..............Self Fabric								
Cancel Date		Ship Date		Delivery Date					
				Origin					
				Created 10 Jan 07 11:04 PM		ADMINISTRATOR			
				Revised 08 Feb 07 10:29 PM		ADMINISTRATOR			

United States Dollar   **Combination Average Cost**

Material	Subtotal	%	Fixed Ovhd	Adj SubTot	Labor	Subtotal	% Ovhd	Fixed Ovhd	Adj SubTot
Fabric	2.113			2.113	Direct				
Trim	1.310			1.310	Contractor				
Others					Dutiable				
Dutiable					**Labor Tot**				
Material Tot	3.423			3.423					

Misc Costs	Subtotal	% Ovhd	Fixed Ovhd	Adj SubTot	Combined	Subtotal	% Ovhd	Fixed Ovhd	Adj SubTot
Sewing	1.750			1.750	Material	3.423			3.423
Cutting	0.300			0.300	Labor				
					Misc.	2.050			2.050
					Accrued	Subtotal	% Ovhd	Fixed Ovhd	Adj SubTot
					Total	5.473			5.473
					Factory	Subtotal	% Ovhd	Fixed Ovhd	Adj SubTot	SAM/SAH
Misc Tot	2.050			2.050					

Adj Total Cost	Sell Price	Margin Margin %	Calc Margin Amt	Cost Diff
5.473	14.990	63.49%	9.518	
5.473	9.950	45.00%	4.478	
5.473	5.473			
				5.473
				5.473

COSTING LAB
Laboratory Applications

1. Explain the difference between cost and price. Give examples; you may wish to use the Internet to support your answer.

2. Robert and Tomé have started their own T-shirt company out of the back of their truck, in Southern California. The shirts are made from vintage tees that are hand-painted by Tomé and sold by Robert. They cater to the beach and surfing crowd. Their T-shirts are very cool and have caught the eye of many California celebrities. Robert and Tomé can now ask any price they like for their shirts, but they cannot keep up with demand; they are finding vintage shirts hard to find and may have to start producing vintage-style shirts, hiring freelance artists to do the painting. They are drawing up a business plan to present to the bank in order to borrow money. They need to figure out how much the shirts will cost to produce.
    a. What steps should Robert and Tomé take in determining how to cost their T-shirts?
    b. Which costing method should they use, and why?

3. Using the cost sheet provided (Figure 2.8), cost out a school project (a garment made in a construction/patternmaking/draping class). (Your instructor may choose to provide a garment instead.) How much would it cost you to manufacture this item? Keep in mind labor in your area. Do not forget to cost the item by the dozen.

4. Advanced students: Using the cost sheet provided, cost out a mini fashion line with six to eight signature pieces. Be sure to include a dress, skirt, pant, and jacket. Once again, do not forget to cost the items by the dozen.

COST SHEET

COMPANY NAME:

ADDRESS:

PHONE:

FAX:

SIZE RANGE:	GARMENT TYPE:	DATE:
MARKERS:	COLORWAY:	STYLE #:
MARKER YARDAGE:	FABRIC CONTENT:	SEASON:
ALLOWANCE:		SELLING PRICE:

MATERIAL COSTS

TYPE OF MATERIALS	YARDS	PRICE	AMOUNT
Fabric			
Contrast			
Lining			
Interfacing			

TRIMMING COSTS

TRIMMINGS	QUAN-TITY	PRICE	AMOUNT
Buttons			
Snaps			
Zippers			
Elastic			
Appliqué/Motifs			
Pads			
Labels/Size tickets			
Polybags			

LABOR COSTS

TYPES OF LABOR	ESTIMATED COST	ACTUAL COST
Cutting		
Sewing		
Grading		
Marking		

OVERHEAD COSTS

TYPES OF OVERHEAD	ESTIMATED COST	ACTUAL COST
Profit		

GARMENT SKETCH

FABRIC SWATCH

ACTUAL COST =

SUGGESTED RETAIL	%	$

Figure 2.8 Cost sheet template.

REFERENCES

Callydus Group LLC. http://callydus.com/.

Glock, Ruth E., and Grace I. Kunz. *Apparel Manufacturing: Sewn Product Analysis*. 2nd ed. Englewood Cliffs, NJ: Prentice Hall, 1995.

Financial Executives International. http://www.financialexecutives.org/ eWeb/DynamicPage.aspx?Site=_fei&WebKey=838a6988-f932-4ef3-9bef-c4e095cd7ca4&reg_evt_key=2bce0a7c-8bab-4853-8fc9-d25fbddb7d1b&paying=Fees.

Harder, Frances. *Fashion for Profit: A Professional's Complete Guide to Designing, Manufacturing, and Marketing a Successful Line*. 8th ed. Rolling Hills Estates, CA: Fashion Business Incorporated, 2008.

"History of Costing Methods." *Encyclopedia of Business Online*. 2nd ed. http://www. referenceforbusiness.com/encyclopedia/Cos-Des/Costing-Methods-Manufacturing. html#HISTORY_OF_COSTING_METHODS.

Keiser, Sandra J., and Myrna B. Garner. *Beyond Design: The Synergy of Apparel Production Development*. 2nd ed. New York: Fairchild Publications, 2008.

Moin, David. "Cost-Cutting beyond the Obvious." *WWD*, July 8, 2008. http://www. wwd.com/retail-news/cost-cutting-beyond-the-obvious-1610851#/article/retail/ news/ cost-cutting-beyond-the-obvious-1610851?full=true.

Pesonen, Lasse T. "Implementation of Design to Profit in a Complex and Dynamic Business Content." PhD dissertation, University of Oulu, 2001.

"Product Cost." The Blueprint Project, University of Hertfordshire. http://www.ider. herts.ac.uk/school/courseware/costs/product_costs.html (accessed on April 3, 2009).

Production Planning and Scheduling

3

SHORT-TERM AND LONG-TERM PLANNING

Planning can be one of the most demanding challenges the production manager meets, as controlling daily aspects of a business requires a great deal of experience and organization. Many studies have shown that organizations should have formal plans; those that do generally show higher profits and higher return on profits as well as other positive financial results (Robbins and Decenzo 2004). These studies also revealed that better planning leads to higher performance (Robbins and Decenzo 2004).

The best way to describe the two major types of business plans is by their time frame, or period (length of time).

The two types of business planning are:

- short-term planning
- long-term planning

Short-term planning is tactical, or operational, and is based on customers' orders. Its goals generally do not extend beyond 1 year. **Long-term planning**, on the other hand, is strategic in nature and often extends beyond 5-year goals. It is based on forecasts and budgets establishing organization-wide objectives.

Planning is necessary to:

- maintain quality
- maintain/increase production facilities
- meet shipping deadlines

Each is dependent on another in its own way. Anyone who has worked in production will tell you that poor planning can be disastrous, resulting in poor quality or damaged merchandise, late goods, or goods missing altogether. A good team will integrate both the company's long- and short-term goals into the overall production plan. (See Table 3.1.)

Short-term planning is appropriate for production, specifically garment production, in which goods are produced several seasons a year. Short-term planning is strategic, creating specific plans that have clearly defined objectives that leave no room for misinterpretation. These plans drive the organization's efforts to achieve its goals. A sequence of standing operations, procedures, standards,

OBJECTIVES

- Understand the differences between long-term and short-term planning.

- Understand the differences between preproduction and production planning.

- Understand the importance of scheduling.

Adapted from Stephen
P. Robbins and David A.
Decenzo. *Fundamentals
of Management: Essential
Concepts and Application.*
4th ed. Upper Saddle
River, NJ: Pearson
Prentice Hall, 2004.

TABLE 3.1 **Production Plans**

TIME FRAME	TYPE	CONDITION	REPETITION
Short-term	Tactical	Specific	Standing
Long-term	Strategic	Directional	Single use

and requirements is essential to the planning process. A knowledge of plant capacity, productivity, and workflow as well as potential bottlenecks can help the production manager make a plan that will work. As work is planned, it is scheduled into one or more factories for production (processing/operation). Too much or too little work in any one factory may impede the flow. The production planner must therefore work closely with sales to keep orders in sync.

Long-term planning should be used for the company—for the manufacturer as a whole or the retailer. Long-term planning involves more complex tactical strategies that anticipate future sales, allowing for future requirements, resources, capacity, and fulfillment. A Materials Requirements Planning (MRP) system— software that is based on production planning and inventory control and that manages manufacturing processes—is used. Long-term plans give the company direction for the objectives it is trying to achieve. Future plans might include a single-use plan of sale, acquisition, or focusing on green initiatives, for example.

PREPRODUCTION AND PRODUCTION PLANNING

Preproduction planning—the process of coordinating the premanufacturing operations to be performed by different functions and workstations—is imperative to meeting delivery dates. By the time the line has hit this point in the process, samples are already approved and costed. Major planning must begin.

The preproduction department coordinates the following tasks:

ORDERING FABRIC FOR DUPLICATE SAMPLES

If the fabric is coming from a different country or from a vendor other than the one that is constructing the garments, extra lead time will be needed for shipping.

CHECKING TO SEE THAT PRODUCTION SAMPLES AND PATTERNS ARE MADE

Samples must be checked by spec technicians or quality control agents for fit and final specs must be approved before patterns are made.

ENSURING THAT PATTERNS ARE GRADED

Patterns are usually graded on Product Data Management (PDM) systems; however, a check that the patterns are complete is necessary.

MAKING SURE SPECIFICATION SHEETS AND TECH-PACKS ARE BEING WORKED ON

The technical packages will go with the final order; each member of the team should be working on his or her part.

Production planning is the next step in processing goods to be produced for sale. **Production planning** involves coordinating plant capacity with style requirements, projected volume, and shipping dates (Glock and Kunz 1995).

Production planning can be accomplished using one of two methods:

- **Cut to order**
- **Cut to stock**

The cut-to-order method is the safer of the two. Companies can rely on orders already placed and add a percentage onto sales for late orders. Companies will cut to stock to fill production time or because of fabric commitments. Companies also use this method for basic styles that are repeated from season to season; however, this is risky, and a company can end up with goods that may not sell.

BOX 3.1 **Industry Insiders David Greenberg and Joe Campinell**

David Greenberg and Joe Campinell, of L'Oréal USA, were in attendance at the 2009 planning meeting of the National Association of Chain Drug Stores (NACDS). The general consensus at this meeting was that although many merchants are lowering their inventory, larger manufacturers are not lowering production.

Greenberg joined L'Oréal in 1993. He has had various roles, including vice president of marketing for hair colorants and hair care at L'Oréal Paris. During his years at L'Oréal, Greenberg took responsibility for the business direction of many of its divisions, which involved strategic planning. As the current president of Maybelline New York, he is assessing the brand and its place in the market. Maybelline mascara products rank at the top, allowing production to flow; however, in the lipstick category, the company is not as fortunate—that product ranks fourth. Of the mascara, Mr. Greenburg states, "This is what happens when you bring innovation and excitement and a little bit of sexiness" (Nagel 2009). Lipstick draws this response: "I don't think we have brought the highest level of innovation there. Over the last five years, our channel of distribution has been losing market share of lip color to specialty stores. You drive the consumer to where the interest, excitement and innovation is, so we haven't done our job" (Nagel 2009).

Campinell works closely with Greenburg and has been the president of L'Oréal USA's consumer products division since 1997. Prior to his current position, Campinell was responsible for the strategic planning and business direction of many of L'Oréal's divisions. Campinell began his 28-year career in the beauty industry, with various positions at Colgate-Palmolive and Chesebrough-Pond.

Figure 3.1

The Polo Ralph Lauren iPhone application allows consumers to use their camera phones to make purchases and view exclusive video content.
Source: Photo courtesy of Women's Wear Daily.

This is a topic that is often discussed at conferences and annual meetings (Box 3.1). Now the actual production planning may begin.

The production department coordinates the following tasks.

NEGOTIATING FABRIC AND FINAL GARMENT COSTS

Depending on the size of the order, the manufacturer may ask for a volume discount for both the fabric order and the labor costs.

CHECKING FINAL SAMPLES AND PROTOTYPES

If final samples were requested (in short lead time they are often skipped), they must be checked against the specs and approved.

INSPECTING PATTERNS AND GRADES

A representative at the manufacturer or vendor's factory will check the patterns and pattern grades for accuracy.

ASSIGNING PRODUCTION CONTRACTS TO VENDORS; INSPECTING FACTORIES

Contracts are assigned to vendors; if needed, final inspections of facilities are made to ensure production capabilities.

FINALIZING TECH-PACKS

Sent with the orders are the technical packages, which include specification sheets.

As new technology advances and more retailers take advantage of **Quick Response Manufacturing (QRM)**, a technique for lean operations, and **Quick Response Delivery System (QR)**, a business strategy that helps retailers shorten the time cycle to get garments to the right place at the right time (thus meeting customer expectations), production planning is made easier. Although these systems work better for basic items, such as underwear, than for high fashion (Levy and Weitz 1998), large retailers, such as Saks Fifth Avenue, have been using the Quick Replenishment system since the mid-1990s for merchandise such as Coach handbags and Donna Karan apparel. Trendsetting designers and manufactures are experimenting with the QR system, forgoing retail operations altogether by selling directly to their customers via the iPhone and other Internet channels (Figure 3.1).

Following are the advantages of QRM:

SAVING TIME

QRM addresses the non-obvious reasons time is used and how it influences total operating costs. QRM also looks at saving time by minimizing, eliminating, or combining procedures.

RESTRUCTURING

QRM restructures the organization to minimize lead time throughout the production cycle. QRM also measures and track performance and data.

ASSESSING SYSTEM DYNAMICS

The system reconsiders capacity-planning policies and the interaction between machines, people, and products.

IMPROVING RESOURCES

QRM looks at the availability and accessibility of resources through purchasing and supply-chain management.

SCHEDULING

Once planning is complete, orders must be assigned to factories. **Scheduling** is necessary in order for a production facility to know what to make, when, where (if it owns, or contracts to, more then one plant), on which equipment, and by how many employees. In other words, the schedule lists what has to be done, by whom, and when. This helps manufacturers and vendors control their time, maximize efficiency, and reduce costs.

TABLE 3.2   Women's Market—Planning Schedule for Five Seasons

JAN	FEB	MAR	APRIL	MAY	JUNE	JULY	AUG	SEPT	OCT	NOV	DEC
		Produce and ship: **summer**	Produce and ship: **summer**								
			Produce and ship: **fall**	Produce and ship: **fall**							
				Produce and ship: **fall II** and **winter**	Produce and ship: **fall II** and **winter**			Finalize, produce: **holiday/ resort**	Produce and ship: **holiday/ resort**		
Produce and ship: **spring**											Produce and ship: **spring**
		Europe *prêt-a-porter:* **spring**							Europe *prêt-a-porter:* **fall**		

Adapted from Sandra J. Keiser and Myrna B. Garner. *Beyond Design: The Synergy of Apparel Production Development.* 2nd ed. Fairchild Publications, 2008.

The parts of the schedule are:

- order dates
- sequence of orders placed
- start dates
- completion dates
- production assignment
- shipping deadlines.

The women's wear market is typically broken into six distinct seasons, not including the European prêt-à-porter (high fashion) lines (Table 3.2). As a result, lines often overlap seasons, with preorders and reorders, making precise scheduling even more important.

To aid in advancing production scheduling, models and program evaluations have been developed to analyze and review techniques. A popular program evaluation and review technique is called simply PERT. It is a flowchartlike technique that has the manager follow three simple principles:

1. *Events*
The completion of major activities; asks the question, "What is the outcome of each activity?"

2. *Activities*
Actions that take place; asks the questions, "What are all the components of the schedule, and how do they affect the progress of production?"

3. *Critical paths*
Taking the longest and most time-consuming activity on the schedule and completing it in the shortest amount of time; asks the question, "What affect will shortening the most time-consuming task have on quality, morale, or the overall schedule?"

The production manager knows the importance of always striving to shorten the lead time in production to save the company money. Working with the sales team, who in turn work with their buyers, is one way. Adding "slack time" (time between a critical path and all other actions) into the schedule is another, because slippage will happen. The schedule will fall at some point, and if it does not, the manager will be happy to have the merchandise delivered early.

PRODUCTION PLANNING AND SCHEDULING LAB
Laboratory Applications

1. How does the push-and-pull supply chain (a producer "pushes" an item onto a customer, while a customer is "pulled" toward an item) affect the planning process? Give examples to support your answer.

2. Miriam and Bob Wright own a small chain of department stores in the northeastern part of the country. For them to stock a variety of styles, they have to limit their stock to one garment per size. They have installed the QR system to make purchasing and stock replenishing quicker and easier.
   a. Are Miriam and Bob smart in limiting their stock to one garment per size in order to carry more items, or should they carry less variety and more stock of each item? Support your answer.
   b. If a customer comes into Bob and Miriam's store, generally liking what they carry, but finds her size is sold out on a number of items, what would you suggest she do, and why?

3. Research and write a short paper (two to three pages) about the QR system. How has it changed the way retailers do business?

4. Vincent has just been promoted into the scheduling department from Reception. He doesn't know much about scheduling, but the owner of the company sees that he is smart and wants to give him a chance. What is the first thing Vincent should learn, and why?

REFERENCES

Beaudry, Jennifer Ernst. "Collective Brands Goes Green for Spring." *WWD Fashion*, March 16, 2009. http://www.wwd.com/footwear-news/collective-brands-goes-green-for-spring-2071664.

Brookman, Faye, and Andrea Nagel. "Hard Times Hit NACDS Annual." *WWD Beauty*, April 24, 2009. http://www.wwd.com/beauty-industry-news/hard-times-hit-nacds-annual-2112244.

Glock, Ruth E., and Grace I. Kunz. *Apparel Manufacturing: Sewn Product Analysis*. 2nd ed. Englewood Cliffs, NJ: Prentice Hall, 1995.

Harder, Frances. *Fashion for Profit: A Professional's Complete Guide to Designing, Manufacturing, and Marketing a Successful Line*. 8th ed. Rolling Hills Estates, CA: Fashion Business Incorporated, 2008.

Karinzadeh, Mark. "Ralph Lauren Collections Head to iPhones." *WWD Fashion*, February 24, 2009. http://www.wwd.com/markets-news/ralph-lauren-collections-head-to-iphones (accessed April 8, 2009).

Keiser, Sandra J., and Myrna B. Garner. *Beyond Design: The Synergy of Apparel Production Development*. 2nd ed. New York: Fairchild Publications, 2008.

Kunz, Grace I., and Myrna B. Garner. *Going Global*. New York: Fairchild Publications, 2007.

Levy, Michael, and Barton A. Weitz. *Retailing Management*. 3rd ed. New York: Richard D. Irwin, 1998.

L'Oréal USA, Inc. Executive Profile. http://www.lorealusa.com/_en/_us/index.aspxdirect1=00001&direct2=00001/00006 (accessed June 16, 2009).

Nagel, Andrea. "Maybelline Adds Sheen to Lip Category with Color Sensational." *WWD*, April 17, 2009. http://www.wwd.com/beauty-industry-news/maybelline-adds-sheen-to-lip-category-with-color-sensational-2107438.

Robbins, Stephen P., and David A. Decenzo. *Fundamentals of Management: Essential Concepts and Applications.* 4th ed. Upper Saddle River, NJ: Pearson Education, 2004.

"What Is Quick Response Manufacturing? A Powerful Method for Slashing Lead Times in All Your Operations!" Center for Quick Response Manufacturing, University of Wisconsin–Madison. http://www.engr.wisc.edu/centers/cqrm/whatisqrm.htm.

Global Production

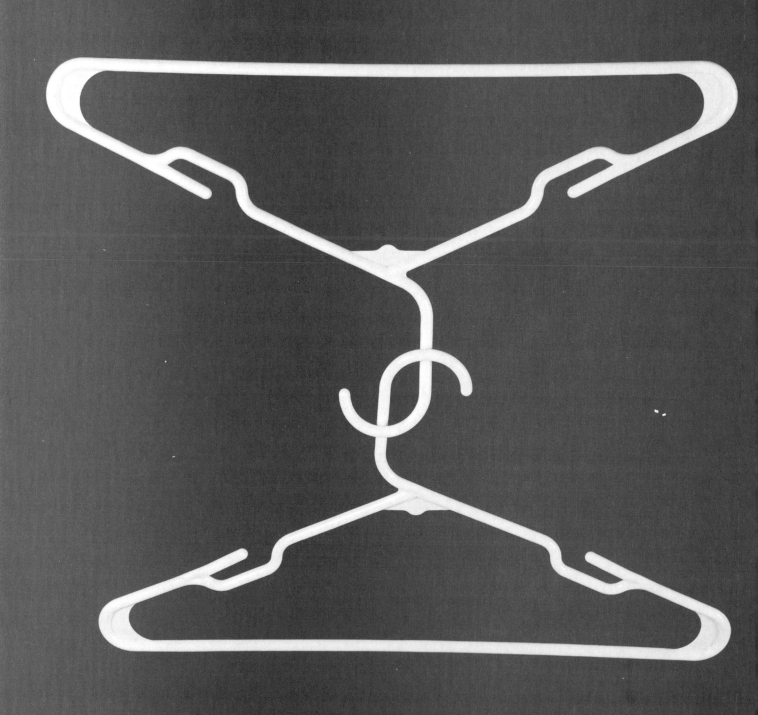

PART TWO

Sourcing Production

4

GLOBAL SOURCING AND THE SOURCING AGENT

Global sourcing is the process of identifying, evaluating, negotiating, and configuring supply across multiple geographies in order to reduce costs, maximize performance, and mitigate risks. A structure is formed, linking raw goods suppliers, manufacturers, factory vendors, and, ultimately, retailers (Figure 4.1, next page). The role of a **sourcing agent** is to carry out the production plan in a reliable and cost-efficient way. The sourcing agent may work for the manufacturer or as a consultant who is paid a fee for bringing the manufacturer and buyer together. The sourcing agent's main goal is to produce items according to quality and engineering specifications. A corporate business plan and merchandising plan will provide direction and will build a solid foundation for the agent. Many buyers and manufacturers go to sourcing shows to find the right agent for their companies.

The duties of a sourcing agent include the following:

1. *Choosing a country or firm (factory), or both, to manufacture goods based on these factors:*
   Quality of goods manufactured
   Availability of materials
   Production capacity
   Ability to meet delivery deadlines
   Efficient service
   Existing quotas or tariffs
   Military issues within country or bordering countries
   Labor practices
   Ability to negotiate good prices

2. *Working as a liaison between the manufacturer, factory (vendor), and retailer by executing the following tasks:*
   Placing orders, handling currency issues, and paying suppliers
   Inspecting factories prior to production for quality and ethical practices
   Facilitating factory visits for manufacturing buyers, spec technicians, and quality-control personnel to visit factories
   Following up with factory online quality control; inspecting finished goods before shipping
   Updating the production team and buyers on product status

NEW GLOBAL SOURCING STRUCTURE

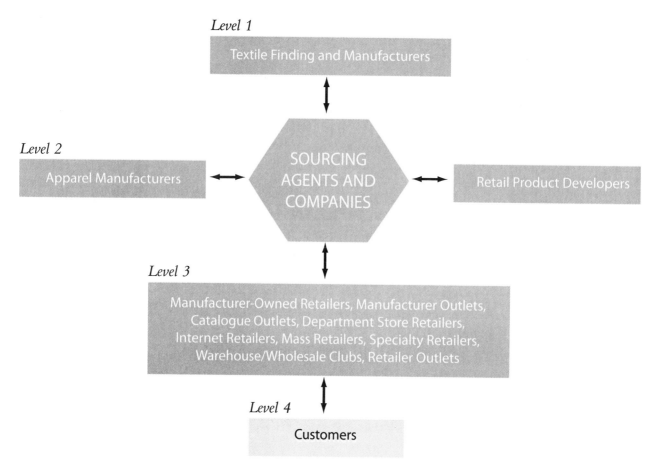

Level 1

Textile Finding and Manufacturers

Level 2

Apparel Manufacturers

SOURCING AGENTS AND COMPANIES

Retail Product Developers

Level 3

Manufacturer-Owned Retailers, Manufacturer Outlets, Catalogue Outlets, Department Store Retailers, Internet Retailers, Mass Retailers, Specialty Retailers, Warehouse/Wholesale Clubs, Retailer Outlets

Level 4

Customers

Figure 4.1

The four levels on this model represent the traditional structure of the fashion industry, organized from textiles and finding down to the consumer. Once sourcing agents had limited contact in the industry; now they can work with almost everyone on every level, except the consumer.

Source: Adapted from Ruth E. Glock, and Grace I. Kunz. Apparel Manufacturing: Sewn Product Analysis, *4th ed. Upper Saddle River, NJ: Prentice Hall, 2005.*

With newer technology and an industry that is so globalized, many factories have been able to focus on efficiency. At the 2009 *WWD* Sourcing & Supply Chain Leadership Forum, conference leaders spoke of the need for sourcing agents to change their focus in the coming years. David Schwarz, of Redcats USA, was one of the leaders who spoke about issues related to sourcing (Box 4.1).

New areas of focus for sourcing agents include the following:

- Dealing with deflation of the world currency
- Handling geographic and economic dynamics, accentuated by a world oversupply of manufacturing capabilities and falling consumer spending
- Finding value beyond capturing the lowest price
- Accepting social responsibility, including protectionism at home and abroad
- Sourcing and managing risk in war-torn or "hot spot" countries
- Dealing with environmental issues
- Incorporating and funding corporate social responsibility programs

Manufacturers can no longer rely on business to boom and profits to soar as they once did. It is imperative that the manufacturer keep track of each phase of the process and understand the risks.

Following are sourcing factors to understand when balancing a business:

- *Material costs*—All prices, including setup tools, transactions, and other costs, related to the actual products or services
- *Transportation costs*—All transportation costs, freight fees, and fuel surcharges
- *Inventory carrying costs*—All warehousing and handling fees, taxes, insurance, depreciation, shrinkage, and other costs associated with maintaining inventories
- *Cross-border taxes, tariffs, and duty costs*—All "landed" costs, including, duties, shipping, and insurance
- *Operational performance*—All costs associated with noncompliance, underperformance, or breach of contract
- *Operational risks*—All costs associated with regional political factors, including change in leadership, war, terrorism, natural disasters, tariff or policy changes, and even widespread disease, that cause a disruption in the supply line

If sourcing agents and manufacturers maintaining a supply mix stay current on market conditions and market intelligence, and then make adjustments as needed using all the tool available to them for analyzing global production, they can minimize their risk and maximize performance. The ultimate goal is to reduce production time, thereby increasing profits.

BOX 4.1   Industry Insider David Schwarz

While being two of the world's cheapest sourcing markets, Bangladesh and Pakistan each carry a separate and "distinct set of risks" (Tucker 2009); this, according to David Schwarz, the vice president of merchandise support and global sourcing for Redcats USA. Schwarz spoke at the *WWD* Sourcing and Supply Chain Leadership Forum in April 2009 on the perils involved with his company's increased reliance on direct sourcing (Ban-gladesh: natural disasters; Pakistan: increasing terror threats). At the time of his talk, Pakistan was the top supplier for Redcats.

Prior to working at Redcats, Schwarz was a department store manager, vice president/general merchandise manager, and chief operating officer for the French department store Printemps. He holds degrees from Ecole Nationale Supérieure des Mines de Paris and École Polytechnique.

PRODUCTION CAPABILITIES

Many manufactures look for factories in regions of the world that specialize, or have expertise, in certain skills. For example, China is known for its silk, Portugal for its cotton flannel; Pakistan and Bangladesh carry some of the lowest labor costs available. The factories and labor forces that make textiles and support garments also have varying technical capabilities from season to season. Output at any given time is mainly affected by four factors. The four major effects on a plant's **production capabilities** are as follows:

1. *Growing season of raw goods*
2. *Weather or natural disasters*
3. *Size of factory/workforce*
4. *Military issues*

It is important to make sure not only that individual factories can produce a company's goods according to plan but also that there are several factories around the globe in the sourcing mix. Keiser and Gardner (2008) note that the following locales offer their own particular capabilities:

- **South Korea, Hong Kong, Taiwan**—High-quality goods
- **Latin America (overall)**—Quick response time
- **Peru**—Sweater manufacturing
- **United States**—Short runs and reorders
- **Pakistan and Bangladesh**—Lower costs

Specialization can impose limits on a factory's capabilities. Some production plants limit the types of garments they produce (Figure 4.2), the sewing procedures they use, and the equipment they have.

Figure 4.2

The 80-year-old Southwick plant in Haverhill, Massachusetts, which specializes in manufacturing suits, now produces only tailored clothing for Brooks Brothers, its new owner.
Source: Photo by Meghan Colangelo, courtesy of Women's Wear Daily.

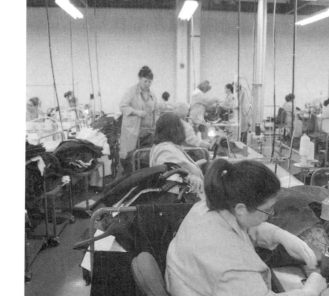

Following are examples of production specialization:

Manufacture Only Certain Product Categories
  Woven shirts and tops
  Knitted garments
  Denim wear and jeans
  Bottoms, including casual pants and skirts
  Dresses
  Children's wear
  Swimwear
  Outerwear

Manufacture Only Garments Made Using Special Equipment
  Embroidered goods
  Knits
  Lace
  Dyed goods
  Acid-wash finishes

Manufacture Only Garments Requiring Specialty-Sewing Capabilities
  Leather goods
  Silk goods
  Foundation apparel

Many factories do their best to stay in the sourcing mix despite their limitations. For example, when a down economy hit the silk industry in China, some factories imported cotton from India. In Pakistan natural gas shortages once hit during winter months, so fabric dying became an operation carried out in summer, when deliveries to the mills are not an issue. Other factories found that cutting their minimum garment order by half or more attracted smaller companies; remaining in the mix is just as important to vendors as it is to suppliers (Figure 4.3).

STYLE ASSIGNMENT AND PRODUCTION SAMPLES

Although it is important for companies to stay diversified, it is equally important for sourcing agents and factory owners to work together building long-term relationships. For manufacturers, the advantage of this type of relationship is reliability, as when new orders or refills need to be filled. For the factory owner, the advantage is continued production flow. Long-term relationships are also helpful in terms of **style assignment**—that is, as styles are assigned to either manufacturer-owned plants or contracted plants.

Figure 4.3

Doo.Ri Chung's lower-priced secondary line Under.Ligne, one of the designer's strategies for surviving economic challenges.

Source: Photo by John Aquino, courtesy of Women's Wear Daily.

Style assignment worksheets are often produced in advance to help prepare production staff. These worksheets are used for:

- meeting market demands and production deadlines
- producing quality garments
- minimizing transfers of goods from plant to plant
- maximizing in-plant efficiencies, using minimum equipment purchases
- ensuring plants are loaded to their operating capacities

To carry out these goals, the worksheets are planned; tracked, using computer software; and managed. Cohen (2009) asserts that whereas vector programs, such as Adobe InDesign and QuarkXPress, are two popular page layout and illustrating programs, Adobe FrameMaker is better for technical documents while, basic programs such as Microsoft Publisher, are well suited for small "low-end" jobs, which rely on desktop printing.

Once a design is chosen, the process begins. New designs and their data are entered into the program, and the technical packages are sent to factories around the world. In general, every design should have a production sample (a firm with its own production plant may choose to forgo this costly process); the contractor or vendors will use this sample as a guide for producing the final garment.

The production sample (Figure 4.4) tells the contractor:

- the right versus the wrong side of the fabric
- where to place topstitching details
- what trims to use
- size-specification verification
- overall quality

The sample also serves as a prototype for the actual production process. It lets the production facility know:

- sewing order
- which production machinery to use
- time needed for each step of production

A production sample can be risky for the manufacturer. Unethical contractors have been known to steal a design and give it to competitors, or, worse, sell the design themselves for a profit. Part of the sourcing agent's job is to have contracted with a reputable source and built a good relationship of mutual trust to avoid such unethical practices.

Figure 4.4

A dress prototype, using washed polyester fabric from the Japanese textile manufacturer Toray Industries, Inc.

Source: Photo by Yukie Kasuga, courtesy of Women's Wear Daily.

SOURCING PRODUCTION LAB
Laboratory Applications

1. What are your thoughts concerning free trade agreements? Have they helped or hurt U.S. manufacturing? Give examples to support your stand.

2. Effie is a freelance sourcing agent who has been working in the Philippines for 15 years. She has a great relationship with several children's wear manufacturers in the states and uses vendors that she knows are reliable and stable. One of her clients asked for a ribbed tank top, and agreed to buy 500,000 units, but wanted to pay only a dollar per shirt. This was a large order for Effie; however, none of her vendors would take the order at that price. Effie found a new plant just outside of Manila and had a sample made. It was shipped to the manufacturer and approved, but at production the quality of the tops was found unacceptable. When Effie inquired, the owner of the factory stated, "It took us 20 tries to get a sample that good—what do you want for a dollar? Cotton is very expensive." The manufacturer in the states canceled the order, and Effie lost the client.
   a. What could Effie have done to ensure better quality from her new vendor?
   b. If none of her other vendors would take the order, why did Effie think this plant could do the job at that price? What should she have done differently?

3. Write a short research paper (three to five pages) on counterfeit goods. Do you think production samples add to the ease of piracy? Use recent news, journal or other trade articles to support your answer.

REFERENCES

Cohen, Sandee. "From Design into Print: Understanding the Types of Computer Applications." Peachpit Press, June 24, 2009. http://www.peachpit.com/articles/article.aspx?p=1352550&seqNum=7 (accessed October 8, 2009).

Gertex Apparel Sourcing Agency International Textile Company. http://www.gertex-textile.com/introducing.html.

Glock, Ruth E., and Grace I. Kunz. *Apparel Manufacturing: Sewn Product Analysis.* 2nd ed. Englewood Cliffs, NJ: Prentice Hall, 1998.

Harder, Frances. *Fashion for Profit: A Professional's Complete Guide to Designing, Manufacturing, and Marketing a Successful Line.* 8th ed. Rolling Hills Estates, CA: Fashion Business Incorporated.

Keiser, Sandra J., and Myrna B. Garner. *Beyond Design: The Synergy of Apparel Production Development.* 2nd ed. New York: Fairchild Publications.

Minahan, Tim. "Global Sourcing: What You Need to Know to Make It Work." SearchCIO.com, August 11, 2003. http://searchcio.techtarget.com/news/article/0,289142,sid182_gci918624,00.html.

Tucker, Ross. "Sourcing Challenges Reach New Heights." *WWD,* April 28, 2009. http://www.wwd.com/markets-news/sourcing-challenges-reach-new-heights-2115653#/slideshow/article/2115653/2115665.

"What is a Sourcing Agent or Buying Agent?" Alibaba.com. http://resources.alibaba.com/topic/10663/What_is_a_Sourcing_Agent_or_Buying_Agent_.htm (accessed April 19, 2009).

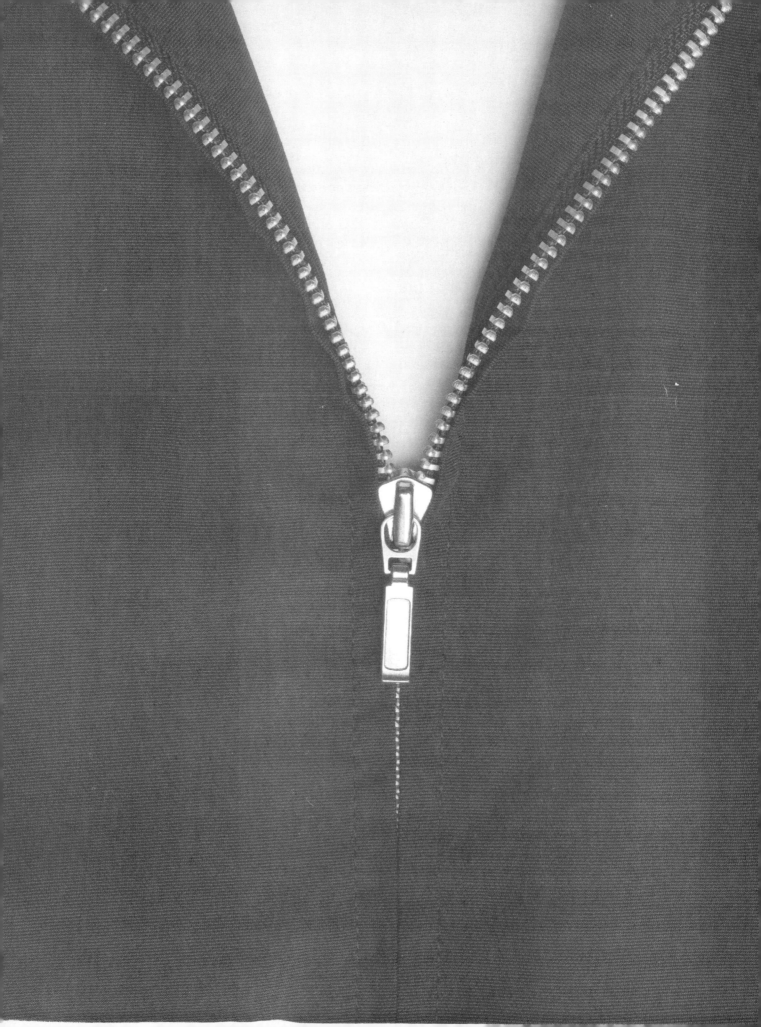

Assembly and Finishing

GARMENT COMPONENTS AND LABOR

Most people who sew at home know garment components as the trims: zippers, buttons, and so on. If you were to look at retail patterns for home sewing, you would see these items listed as components. However, in manufacturing, all parts of the garment are considered components—there is no distinction between body components and trim components. Later, when you learn about the technical package, there will be a fabric sheet and a component/trim sheet (which can be confusing), but on the sewing floor, all parts of the garment are components (Figures 5.1 and 5.2, next page).

Glock and Kunz (1995) state that the basic garment components include

- top fronts and top backs
- bottom fronts and bottom backs
- sleeves
- collars and neckline treatments
- cuffs and sleeve treatments
- plackets
- pockets
- waistline treatments

An entire industry of component suppliers exists to manufacture everything from fibers to fabrics to leathers and furs. There are also suppliers of buttons, zippers, elastic (Figure 5.3), hook-and-eye closures, threads, and more. These are the raw goods and component materials used in garment construction.

Hems, stitches, seams, bonding, or a combination of these, is used to assemble the components. As mentioned previously, production **assembly**—the fitting together of all the **garment components**, or smaller parts, into a complete structure—is determined when making the sample garment (see Chapter 4). The more components a garment has, the more complex the assembly and the higher the labor costs.

There are three methods of assembly and therefore of paying labor:

- Progressive bundle system
- Unit production system
- Modular production system

OBJECTIVES

- Understand garment components and labor.

- Understand the relationship between components and assembly.

- List the steps in garment finishing.

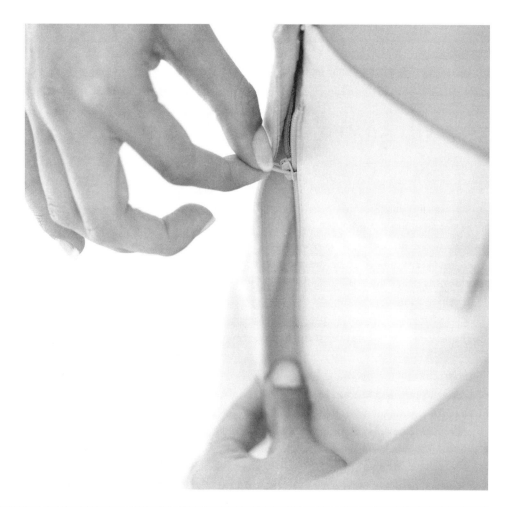

Figure 5.1

A classic zipper component
on the sewing floor would be
one of many parts.
Source: © Masterfile
(Royalty-Free Division).

Figure 5.2

On the sewing floor, all
parts of the garment are
components.
Source: Julian Ward/
Getty Images.

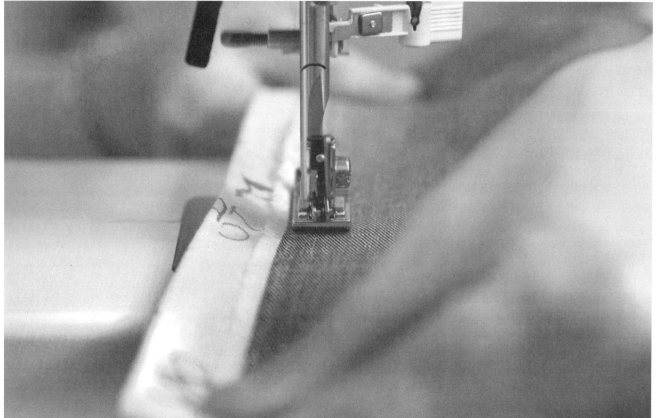

The progressive bundle system (PBS) is the most traditional. After being cut in the cutting room, various components are tied into bundles, with smaller pieces attached to larger, and sewn in a progression. Each operator is paid piecework, or by the bundle; this is called the SAM (standard allowed minutes) system. The operators are encouraged to work quickly and to produce quantity, but quality can suffer because individuals may work at different rates, with different degrees of expertise, or even because of equipment failure. Some factories have porters—helpers who transport the bundles from station to station—but often the operators will have to stop, leave the workstation, and move goods themselves (Figure 5.4).

Unfortunately, PBS has proven to be an ineffective practice for production managers and factory operators alike: it is difficult to plan and manage effectively. PBS often requires more overtime, as operators do makeup and repair work on unfinished operations. However, with newer technology and automated machinery, the success of the system is improving.

With the unit production system (UPS), also known as the overhead conveyer system, garment components are loaded into a transporter, or conveyer, that moves them from one operator to the next (Figure 5.5). In some instances the operator does not even need to remove the garment from the conveyer system in order to complete his or her task, as the conveyer is designed to position the component as needed. Upon competition of assembly, the component arrives at the unloading station, and the empty carrier returns for loading. Pay is based on the total number of garments completed. Unfortunately, seconds and subpar garments are removed from the line, which often reduces the workers' total pay.

Figure 5.3

A colorful waistband on a pair of Calvin Klein trunks.
Source: Photo by Thomas Iannaccone, courtesy of Women's Wear Daily.

Figure 5.4

Bundles waiting to be assembled at the Evans Group, a fashion development and production house, in Oakland, California.
Source: Photo by Kristen Loken, courtesy of Women's Wear Daily.

TABLE 5.1   **Description of Garment**

Top fronts and top backs—These are the major sections of the top portion of a garment that determine the basic silhouette, style, and shape. They may consist of one or more pieces, depending on the styling, and usually mirror image left to right (front or back), unless asymmetrical. Generally, these pieces have other smaller components attached during construction, before the garment is assembled.

Bottom fronts and bottom backs—These are the major sections of the bottom portion of a garment that determine the basic silhouette, style, and shape. They may consist of one (skirts only) or more pieces, depending on the styling and usually mirror image left to right (front or back), unless asymmetrical. Generally, these pieces have other smaller components attached during construction, before the garment is assembled.

Sleeves—These components are not only functional for covering the arms but also add to the design, style, and silhouette of the garment. Additional components, such as plackets and cuffs, may be added before the sleeves are attached to the garment or after, depending on assembly line needs.

Collars and neckline treatments—Collars, knitted bands, facings, ribs, and plackets are all examples of neckline treatments that are added to the top front and back components. These smaller components are generally attached before the garment is assembled and add aesthetic appeal.

Cuffs and sleeve treatments—Cuffs, casings, facings, ribs, and hems are all components or treatments used to finish off a sleeve. They vary with styling and garment function, and may be sewn to the sleeve before being attached to the garment or after.

Plackets—Plackets are a finished edge or opening on a garment that allows a body part to pass through. Depending on placement, a placket generally requires a closure. The placket is often attached early in the assembly process. Plackets vary in design and quality and thus cost as well.

Pockets—Pockets may add a design or functional element to a garment, or both. Depending on the pocket type, they may be sewn onto the body component before assembly (patch or welt pockets) or they may be part of the assembly process (side-seam pockets).

Waistline treatments—Bands, ribbing, casings, facings, and elastic are all components used to create waistline treatments. With the exception of a one-piece garment, waist treatments are often saved for the end of the assembly process, as they finish the top of the garment edge, defining the waist and holding the garment in place.

Ruth E. Glock and Grace I. Kunz. *Apparel Manufacturing: Sewn Product Analysis*. 2nd ed. Eaglewood Cliffs, NJ: Prentice Hall, 1995.

Figure 5.5

Garments move on a
conveyer, while a woman
works at a station inside
the Max Mara factory in
Reggio Emilia, Italy.
*Source: Photo by Dave Yoder,
courtesy of* Women's Wear Daily.

The advantage of UPS for the production manager is that all the pieces of one complete product travel together (e.g., for a skirt: the front, backs, waistband, pockets, and so on). Any small components, such as the zipper or buttons used to finish a skirt or pant, are usually stored at each station throughout the process or can hang with the garment. The end result is a system that reduces overtime and is cost-efficient.

The modular production system (MPS) is the newest of the three systems. It focuses on a team method of assembly. The members are responsible for either the entire garment process or a specific station, depending on the overall plant operations. The team is trained on the functions required and paid as a team, based on total output; team members still operate individual machines and do separate tasks, but they work together for their final compensation. They are also cross-trained, which helps the company avoid production backups.

MPS has proven successful in reducing seconds and improving quality. There have been indications that greater job satisfaction has added to improved job performance. In addition, Abend (1999) reported fewer job-related injuries, as workers are rotated from task to task, cutting down on repetition.

Labor—the physical work involved in producing goods—is one of the most expensive aspects of production. A global study released by the U.S. consulting firm Jassin-O'Rourke and published by EmergingTextiles.com shows countries such as Bangladesh, Cambodia, Pakistan, Vietnam, and China offering a labor pay scale ranging from 22 cents to 1 dollar and 8 cents an hour—prices the United States cannot begin to compete with ("Apparel Manufacturing Labor Costs" 2008).

Labor costs include:

- **bundling**
- **sewing**
- **pressing**
- **trimming**
- **inspection**

How the garments are assembled, which method of assembly is used, how experienced the operators are, how efficiently the plant is run, and the technological advances within the plant will all affect labor costs. Production managers look at each and every factor to reduce costs, saving money and increasing profits. Assembly-line production is one of the major places a manager looks to reduce cost.

THE COMPONENT–ASSEMBLY RELATIONSHIP

In assembly-line production, there is always more than one way to put together a garment. For example, the pocket of a blazer may be added to the breast piece before it is sewn to any of the other garment components, or it may be added at the end, in the small component or finishing process.

The progression of assembly (Figure 5.6) is often based on these factors:

- **Total number of garment components**
- **Assembly methods**
- **Types of stitches and seams required**
- **Types of machinery available**
- **Degree of automation**
- **Pressing methods**
- **Overall capacity of the plant**

The production manager will assess the efficiency of goods moving through the plant when making decisions about materials handling, or the entire process of garment assembly. The finishing process is also factored into the assembly production.

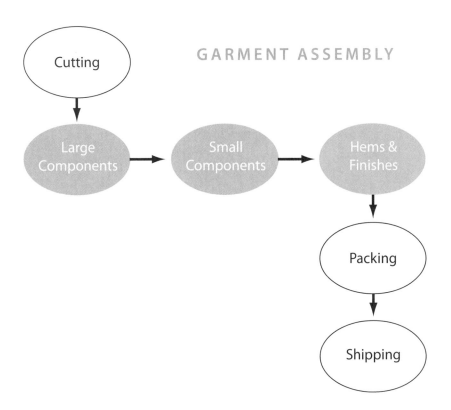

GARMENT ASSEMBLY

Cutting → Large Components → Small Components → Hems & Finishes → Packing → Shipping

Figure 5.6

Garment assembly; separate pieces join to create a unit.

FINISHING

In apparel, **finishing** is the process that gives the garment its saleable appearance. Like the other methods of production, finishing can be automated, using UPS, or can employ the older PBS. Either way, the operations for finishing can be broken into two distinct phases:

1. **Garment finishing**—The last steps to completing the garment; garment finishing is further broken down into the following steps (Figure 5.7):

   > Final sewing operations (buttons, hems, and so on)
   > Trimming treads
   > Dyeing garments
   > Wet finishes
   > Final pressing
   > Final inspections

2. **Packing**—This is also included in the finishing process and may include the following elements (Figure 5.8):

   > Labels
   > Tickets
   > Hangtags
   > Folding or hanging
   > Plastic (poly) bagging
   > Packing (cardboard box or hanging rack)

Now that the garments have been finished and packed, they are ready for shipping—a goal Luigi Maramotti looks forward to achieving each season (Box 5.1).

BOX 5.1 **Industry Insider Luigi Maramotti**

As chief executive officer of the 1.4-billion dollar Max Mara Group, Luigi Maramotti believes that the link between a precision-cut coat and abstract art might not be obvious, but that each in their own way, art and fashion exist in "the same type of climate, the same changes" (Ilari 2009).

Maramotti is much like his late father, the founder of the company and an art collector; he believes in craftsmanship rather than showmanship, which can be seen in the company's factories. One coat may require 150 steps, from raw fabric to finished product, labored over "by a predominantly female workforce hunched over workbenches like laborious bees" (Ilari 2009). And, unlike companies that have branched out into other product categories, such as beauty, under Maramotti, Max Mara remains rooted, as it always has been, in women's ready-to-wear and accessories: "'The product is our lighthouse, our DNA'" (Ilari 2009).

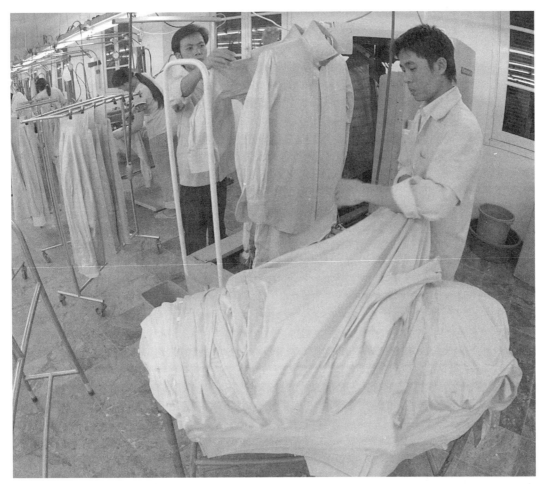

Figure 5.7

Employees feed an ironing machine with shirts as part of the finishing process at the factory of German shirt producer van Laack in Hanoi, Vietnam.
Source: PETER KNEFFEL/ dpa/Landov.

Figure 5.8

An inspector doing a final spot check just before shipping, inside the Max Mara factory in Reggio Emilia, Italy.
Source: Photo by Dave Yoder/ Aurora Photos.

ASSEMBLY AND FINISHING LAB
Laboratory Applications

1. Choose a favorite garment from your closet. How many components does the garment have? Remember to include all parts as well as trims and findings. What do you think is the order (on the assembly line) in which this garment was constructed?

2. Explain which system of assembly (UPS, PBS, MPS) you think works best in today's world, and why. Use data from recent trade journals or Internet articles to support your answer.

3. Sandra owns a midsized children's wear company in Georgia. The garments are made around the world; however, the company has always done the final finishing at the Georgia warehouse, before shipping to retailers in the United States. As the company grows, Sandra wonders if she should continue to finish her goods at the warehouse or have each vendor finish them and use the warehouse just for distribution. What do you think Sandra should do, and why?

4. What are the advantages and disadvantages of each method?

REFERENCES

Abend, Jules. "Modular Manufacturing: The Line between Success and Failure." *Bobbin*, January 1999. http://findarticles.com/p/articles/mi_m3638/is_5_40/ai_55609241/ (accessed October 2, 2009).

"Apparel Manufacturing Labor Costs in 2008." Emerging Textiles.com, May 23, 2008. http://www.emergingtextiles.com/?q=art&s=080523-apparel-labor-cost&r=free.

"The Eton System." http://www.eton.se/TheEtonSystem/TheSystem.htm.

Glock, Ruth E., and Grace I. Kunz. *Apparel Manufacturing: Sewn Product Analysis*. 2nd ed. Englewood Cliffs, NJ: Prentice Hall, 1995.

Harder, Frances. *Fashion for Profit: A Professional's Complete Guide to Designing, Manufacturing, and Marketing a Successful Line*. 8th ed. Rolling Hills Estates, CA: Fashion Business Incorporated, 2008.

Jarnow, Jeannette, and Kitty G. Dickerson. *Inside the Fashion Business*. 6th ed. Upper Saddle River, NJ: Prentice Hall, 1991.

Keiser, Sandra J., and Myrna B. Garner. *Beyond Design: The Synergy of Apparel Production Development*. 2nd ed. New York: Fairchild Publications, 2008.

Kunz, Grace I., and Myrna B. Garner. *Going Global*. New York: Fairchild Publications, 2007.

Rogers, G. G., and L. Bottaci. "Modular Production Systems: A New Manufacturing Paradigm." *International Journal of Intelligent Manufacturing* vol. 8, no. 2 (April 1997): 147–156. http://www.cage.curtin.edu.au/mechanical/modautogp/MPS_paper.htm.

"The Smart MRT Is Indeed a Cost-Saving and Profit-Making Production System." *Fortune City*. web.singnet.com.sg/~smcpl/product/ups/compareups.htm.

"The Stations in the Modular Production System at a Glance." Festo Didactic. http://www.festo-didactic.com/int-en/learning-systems/mps-the-modular-production-system/stations/the-stations-in-the-modular-production-system-at-a-glance.htm.

Packaging and Distribution

6

LABELS, HANGTAGS, AND PACKAGING

Most people today are aware of the impact of labeling. The design of a **label**—its size, type, color, and placement—helps create brand recognition and builds brand loyalty. Yet label information must also meet certain federal regulations—labeling laws that require merchandise to be correctly labeled and displayed (Figure 6.1, next page).

Federal care label requirements include:

- fiber content
- care instructions
- country of origin
- vendor identification (RN number)

Garments may contain as many as three labels: the care label; the manufacturer, or designer, label; and a size label. It is up to the manufacturer to determine if it wants to add size onto the care label; the law does not require it. This also applies to the **hangtag**, the decorative tag attached to an article of merchandise that provides information about its size and cost. Often a manufacturer will use one large hangtag with the company logo on one side and size and style information on the other. Some manufactures, however, prefer to use a two-sided hangtag as a means of increasing brand recognition and then add a smaller tag to carry size and style information. Either way, hangtags are an essential part of marketing and of developing customer loyalty (Figure 6.2).

Bar coding has become an essential part of ticketing in retail. With bar coding, a garment can be priced (preticket) before shipping. The 13-digit bar code instituted in 2005 conforms to international Global Location Number (GLN) standards.

The information contained for apparel (Figure 6.3) includes:

- vendor name
- style number
- color
- size information

OBJECTIVES

- **Understand the role of labels, hangtags, and packaging.**

- **Understand the distribution process.**

CODE OF FEDERAL REGULATIONS

Figure 6.1

For rules and regulations under the Textile Fiber Products Identification Act, go to http://www.ftc.gov/os/statutes/textile/rr-textl.htm.

Figure 6.2

In November 2008 the Ellen Tracy logo and mark updated their look, with two *E*s merging to form a *T*. The new icon is used on hangtags, tissue paper, and tonal prints in linings.

Bar codes help retailers check in shipments, record sales, and track inventory. In addition, two-dimensional (2D) technology, in which symbols are used to encode information instead of bars, is being tested. Sonic Bar and Microsoft Tag have gone live in many countries, including parts of Asia: shoppers can simply point their cell phones at a tag and call up a Web site or video with information. Such information might include, for example, whether a garment was made from sustainable fabrics or via an eco-friendly process. Together, Avery Dennison and Scanbuy have developed similar 2D technology, using Scanbuy's ScanLife application as the basis (Figure 6.4). With it, shoppers can use their camera phones to find matching items and display discounts and other helpful product data from manufacturers.

Packaging is done at the manufacturing (vendor) plants. Most merchandise is shipped ready for retailers' shelves or racks; however, some high-end retailers will change out hangers or refold garments to meet their specific standards. As discussed previously, garments are folded, or hung and placed in polybags, and then placed in cardboard boxes for shipping (see Chapter 5). In an effort to preserve natural resources and comply with local laws, many vendors have switched to recycled cardboard boxes.

Some garments require extra packing. For example, men's dress shirts have collar stays, pins, and tissue paper. Evening gowns may have tissue paper in the bodice or sleeves to keep the dress from crushing during shipping. This extra material will often stay in the garment on the showroom floor to keep it fresh-looking; other garments are packed with special hangers to keep the garments from falling onto the sales floor. The **packaging**, as well as the label and ticket, is designed to give each garment the best visual presentation possible. The intimate apparel retailer Ann Deal knows all too well the importance of packaging (Box 6.1).

THE DISTRIBUTION PROCESS

Distribution—the delivery of merchandise from handling facilities—is the last step in the process. In the retail industry traditional warehouses designed to house inventory are being replaced by much larger and more technologically sophisticated distribution centers.

There are three types of distribution:

1. *Distribution center*
2. *Distribution center bypass*
3. *Cross-docking*

DISTRIBUTION CENTER

A distribution center (DC) is a facility that handles merchandise. Manufacturers who own their own plants may also own their own distribution centers. Retailers who source to vendors may own their own distribution centers or may source centers as well.

DCs are used as locations to:

- monitor goods coming in from vendors
- repack and ship goods to stores
- reinspect or spot-check quality of goods
- analyze returned retail merchandise to determine the source of the problem
- warehouse overruns or unsold goods to be sold at discount or outlet stores

BOX 6.1 Industry Insider Ann Deal

Ann Deal, the owner of Fashion Forms intimate apparel, in California, says packaging is "'different for each retailer, lending an exclusive look, whether it's Frederick's of Hollywood or Walmart'" (Monget 2009).

Ann began her career in the intimates department of Rich's in Atlanta. She has come a long way in expanding her business of intimate apparel accessories, with wholesale sales in excess of $40 million. Her specialty is novelty items, such as the Water Bra and reusable silicone Breast Petals. Her products are sold at big-name retailers, including Walmart, Target, Macy's, Kmart, Sears, and JCPenney stores, as well as the UK retailers Selfridges and British Home Stores.

Why does Ann do what she does? "'It's great to create intimate solutions for women to make their lives easier, more comfortable and more beautiful'" (Monget 2009).

Figure 6.5

Inside a Walmart
distribution center.

Source: Marc F. Henning / Alamy.

The advantages of the DC method (Figure 6.5) are:

- handling large shipments
- warehousing goods in anticipation of season
- offering support departments, such as human resources, accounting, and so on

DISTRIBUTION CENTER BYPASS

Distribution center bypass (DC bypass), also called direct shipping, is a strategy in which vendors ship goods directly to the stores. This newer method may save days, whereas goods might otherwise be sitting at the distribution center.

DC bypass locations are used to:

- receive goods from shipping containers
- inspect goods
- ultimately, ship goods to stores

The advantages of the DC bypass method are:

- inventory reduction
- decreased handling costs
- decreased transportation and fuel costs

CROSS-DOCKING

Cross-docking is a method of unloading goods from one incoming semitrailer truck or railcar onto other, outbound vehicles, with little or no storage in between.

Cross-docking is used to:

- change the type of vehicle/transportation
- sort goods intended for different destinations
- combine goods from different origins

The advantages of the cross-docking method (Figure 6.6) are:

- reduced handling, operating, and warehouse costs
- faster receipt of goods
- inventory reduction, owing to quicker replenishment

Late shipping must be avoided at all costs, no matter which method is used. Retailers can and will cancel orders based on late shipments. This, in turn, can cause manufacturers to be stuck with merchandise they may not be able to sell for a profit.

TYPES OF DISTRIBUTION

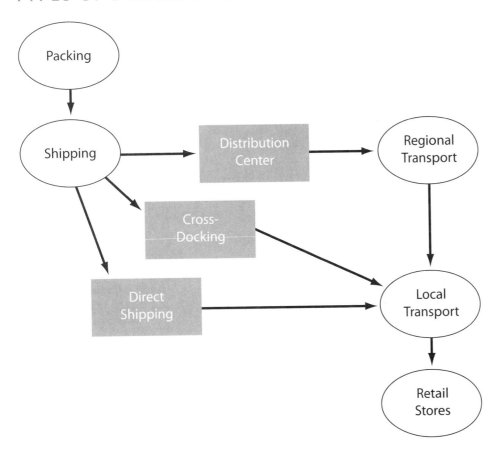

Figure 6.6
Illustrated are the three methods used to distribute goods to retailers.

PACKAGING AND DISTRIBUTION LAB
Laboratory Applications

1. Select a favorite garment from your closet. How many labels does the garment have? What are the contents of each? Do they comply with federal regulations?

2. Design your own hangtag for your garment. Consider what would make it marketable on the retail floor.

3. Aaron and Sabina started a sheepskin boot company on their ranch in Colorado. The company offices and manufacturing facilities are located in their converted barn, with a small adjoining warehouse. So far they have been able to fill orders using UPS- and FedEx-type shipping methods. They would like to expand the line, offering coats and handbags, but will need the current warehouse space for more offices. The coats and handbags will not be made on-site. Aaron would like to build a new warehouse and distribution center at the ranch. Sabina would like to build a new warehouse but continue using their current carriers at the ranch. She wants the coat and handbag merchandise to ship directly from supplier (factory) to customer.

    a. What type of distribution method is Aaron proposing? Is his method best for the company? Why or why not?
    b. What type of distribution method is Sabina proposing? Is her method best for the company? Why or why not?

REFERENCES

"Avery Dennison and Scanbuy, Inc., Introduce Mobile-Merchandising Solution" Scanbuy. http://www.scanbuy.com/web/index.php?option=com_content&view=article&id=58:avery-dennison-and-scanbuy-inc-introduce-mobile-merchandising-solution&catid=2:press-releases&Itemid=6 (accessed May 19, 2009).

Berman, Barry, and Joel. R. Evans. *Retail Management: A Strategic Approach.* 7th ed. Upper Saddle River, NJ: Prentice Hall, 1998.

Glock, Ruth E., and Grace I. Kunz. *Apparel Manufacturing: Sewn Product Analysis.* 2nd ed. Englewood Cliffs, NJ: Prentice Hall, 1995.

Harder, Frances. *Fashion for Profit: A Professional's Complete Guide to Designing, Manufacturing, and Marketing a Successful Line.* 8th ed. Rolling Hills Estates, CA: Fashion Business Incorporated, 2008.

Keiser, Sandra J., and Myrna B. Garner. *Beyond Design: The Synergy of Apparel Production Development.* 2nd ed. New York: Fairchild Publications, 2008.

Kunz, Grace I., and Myrna B. Garner. *Going Global.* New York: Fairchild Publications, 2007.

Monget, Karyn. "Ann Deal Builds on Intimate Accessories." *WWD,* April 6, 2009. http://www.wwd.com/markets-news/ann-deal-builds-on-intimate-accessories-2091609.

Napolitano, Maida. "Warehouse Management: How to Be a Lean, Mean Cross-Docking Machine." *Logistics Management,* January 1, 2007. http://www.logisticsmgmt.com/article/CA6405824.html (accessed October 4, 2009).

————. "Warehousing and Distribution Center Management: The Cross-Dock Revolution: Are You in or Out?" *Logistics Management,* April 1, 2008. http://www.logisticsmgmt.com/article/CA6549333.html (accessed October 4, 2009).

Stone, Elaine. *The Dynamics of Fashion.* New York: Fairchild Publications, 1999.

"When 'Does DC Bypass' Make Sense?" *Supply Chain Digest,* September 8, 2002. http://www.scdigest.com/assets/On_Target/08-09-02-3.php?cid=1894&ctype=content.

The Technical Package

PART THREE

The Technical Package

THE TECHNICAL PACKAGE: OVERVIEW

A **technical package** (tech-pack, TechPack, techpack, or teck pac) is an assemblage of information required by an apparel manufacturer to create, put together, and package a garment. In other words, the tech-pack encompasses all the garment specifications needed before mass production. The package can be simple or complex, depending on the user's needs. The design of a technical package, also known as a production package, varies greatly within the industry. As mentioned previously, parts of the document are prepared in the design department (see Chapter 2). They are finalized in consultation with the merchandisers and then go on to the production department. Ultimately, the production department uses the tech-pack as a reference and guide for bulk manufacturing. Once a tech-pack has received final approval, its use is manifold.

The tech-pack may be used in the following ways:

- The production department can go into the manufacturing process without needing to refer back to the design team.
- Merchandisers and sourcing agents can ensure required materials are made available for production in proper quantities and on time.
- Marketing can use the document in presentations or to sell styles to key customers before line samples are made.
- Various departments within the company can refer to the tech-pack for points of discussion.
- The tech-pack brings unity and efficiency to a company.

OBJECTIVES

- Understand the purpose and uses of a technical package (tech-pack).

- Identify the parts of a basic tech-pack.

- Understand the variety of methods used to build a tech-pack.

BUILDING A TECH-PACK

The complexity of garment style, the size of the company, the software available, and even the personalities of the production manager and designers govern the content of the tech-pack. From the 1-page tech-pack in Figure 7.1 to the 27-page sheets bemoaned by one poster on the blog 39thandbroadway (April 24, 2009), there is no such thing as a standard pack. However, all packs should cover the basics. Part 3 of this text presents several popular industry tech-packs, in addition to a number of original tech-packs representative of those used by industry professionals.

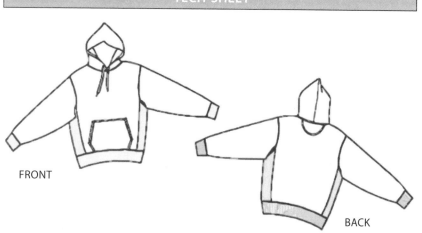

HEAVYWEIGHT PULLOVER HOODED SWEATSHIRT TECH-SHEET

"The Hoodie" by Sport Boy

FRONT

BACK

COLORS

 Black

 Brown

 Red

 Gray

PLEASE NOTE:
Colors shown are for reference only. For closest match, see PMS colors; for exact match, samples are available.

* 12-ounce, 80/20 ring-spun cotton/polyester * Rib-knit side gussets
* Contrast twill tape in neck seam * 2 × 2 rib-knit cuffs and waistband with spandex
* Self-front pouch pocket * 2-ply hood with dyed-to-match lining and drawstring

SIZE	XS	S	M	L	XL	1X	2X	3X
Width	19	21	23	25	27	29	31	33
Length	28	29	30	31	32	33	35	35
Sleeve (CB)	33	35	36	37	38	39	40	41
Neck	10	10.25	10.5	10.75	11	11.5	11.75	12

CARE INSTRUCTIONS:

Machine wash cold. Wash with like colors.
Do not bleach. Tumble dry low.
Warm iron if necessary.

Chest width measured 1" below armhole, across chest. Body length measured from high point, shoulder seam to hem.
Sleeve length measured from center neck to hem, following top edge. Neck width measured from seam to seam.

FABRIC INFORMATION	BLACK	BROWN	RED	GRAY
Textile PMS	19-4010TC	19-1213TC	18-1661-TC	14-3803TC
General PMS	193	9519C	193C	435C

A basic tech-pack (Figure 7.2) includes these components:

DESIGN SHEET

(also known as a product lead or cover sheet)

The design sheet outlines the initial information needed for a specific garment under production.

Figure 7.2a

Sample technical package

design sheet.

DESIGN SHEET	PAGE #01
COMPANY NAME:	STYLE #
ADDRESS:	SKETCH
PHONE:	
FAX:	
GARMENT INFORMATION	
GROUP NAME:	
CLASSIFICATION:	
SEASON:	
GARMENT LABEL:	
FABRIC CONTENT:	
COLORWAY:	
DESCRIPTION:	
	Designer Initials

DATE CREATED:	DATE MODIFIED:	DATE RELEASED:

ILLUSTRATION SHEET   PAGE #02

COMPANY NAME:	STYLE #	
ADDRESS:	GROUP NAME:	
	CLASSIFICATION:	SEASON:
PHONE:	GARMENT LABEL:	
FAX:	COLORWAY:	

SKETCH

Designer Initials

FABRIC INFORMATION	STYLE WIDTH	SIZE RANGES	DELIVERY DATE	COMMENTS

DATE CREATED:	DATE MODIFIED:	DATE RELEASED:

FABRIC SHEET   PAGE #03

COMPANY NAME:	STYLE #	
ADDRESS:	GROUP NAME:	
	CLASSIFICATION:	SEASON:
PHONE:	GARMENT LABEL:	
FAX:	COLORWAY:	
SKETCH	SWATCH	

Designer Initials

FABRIC INFORMATION	STYLE WIDTH	SIZE RANGES	DELIVERY DATE	COMMENTS

DATE CREATED:	DATE MODIFIED:	DATE RELEASED:

COMPONENT SHEET							PAGE #04
COMPANY NAME:			**STYLE #**				
ADDRESS:			**GROUP NAME:**				
			CLASSIFICATION:			**SEASON:**	
PHONE:			**FABRIC CONTENT:**				
FAX:			**COLORWAY:**				

ITEM-VENDOR-CODE-ORIGIN	CONTENT	SIZE-QUANTITY-UNIT OF MEASURE	LOCATION	COLOR	COMMENTS

DATE CREATED:	DATE MODIFIED:	DATE RELEASED:

ILLUSTRATION SHEET
This sheet shows garments in multiple colorways (color scheme) and any other pertinent information.

FABRIC SHEET
The fabric sheet ensures the proper fabric is used in production.

COMPONENT/TRIM SHEET
This sheet makes certain the proper trims and sewing components are used in production.

Figure 7.2b

(top left) Sample technical package illustration sheet.

Figure 7.2c

(bottom left) Sample technical package fabric sheet.

Figure 7.2d

(above) Sample technical package component sheet.

LABEL/PACKING SHEET						PAGE #05
COMPANY NAME:			STYLE #			
ADDRESS:			GROUP NAME:			
			CLASSIFICATION:		SEASON:	
PHONE:			FABRIC CONTENT:			
FAX:			COLORWAY:			
ITEM-VENDOR-CODE-ORIGIN	CONTENT	SIZE-QUANTITY-UNIT OF MEASURE		LOCATION	COLOR	COMMENTS
DATE CREATED:		DATE MODIFIED:			DATE RELEASED:	

Figure 7.2e

Sample technical package
label/packing sheet.

LABEL/PACKING SHEET
The label/packing sheet lists the proper labels, hangtags, hangers, and polybags used in production.

DETAIL/CONSTRUCTION SHEET		PAGE #06	
COMPANY NAME:	**STYLE #**		
ADDRESS:	**GROUP NAME:**		
	CLASSIFICATION:		**SEASON:**
PHONE:	**FABRIC CONTENT:**		
FAX:	**COLORWAY:**		
DETAIL	**DETAIL**		

DATE CREATED:	DATE MODIFIED:	DATE RELEASED:

DETAIL/CONSTRUCTION SHEET

This sheet details proper stitch types, stitch widths, and any other special construction needs.

Figure 7.2f

Sample technical package detail/construction sheet.

SPEC SHEET											PAGE #07

COMPANY NAME:

STYLE #:

ADDRESS:

GROUP NAME:

CLASSIFICATION: SEASON:

PHONE:

LABEL:

FAX:

COLORWAY:

TECHNICAL SKETCH:

SKETCH/PHOTO:

CODE	POINT OF MEASURE	TOL. ±	4 S	6	8	10 M	12	14 L	16	18 XL

COMMENTS:

DATE CREATED: DATE MODIFIED: DATE RELEASED:

Figure 7.2g

Sample technical package

specification sheet.

SPEC SHEET

The spec sheet makes certain each garment meets specific measurements.

INDUSTRY TECH-PACKS

The tech-pack can be built using a number of different software applications. **Product Lifecycle Management (PLM)** is a popular software system, often used in conjunction with **Product Data Management (PDM)** software, to collect, process, and disperse the style data in an electronic filing system. The software is designed to offer updated information at every stage of the development process. This information is produced at the source—that is, the employee who is responsible for a process or procedure enters the corresponding data. As a result, problems and errors can be identified quickly, saving time and costly production mistakes.

The suppliers of PDM and PLM software targeted for technical packages, and aimed at improving the product manufacturing process and reducing costs, are numerous. The PDM Fashion Industry Software Web site profiles more than a dozen such companies. The site lists Gerber Scientific (the parent company of Gerber Technology) as a leader in developing and manufacturing integrated software and hardware automation systems. A company that uses Gerber Technology but offers the program through a freelance site is TechPackCentral (Figure 7.3, pages 82–88). Lectra has had numerous high-profile clients, including Mango, Denim Authority, and JL International. Centric Software, another big name in the industry, has added tech-pack design to its line, filling a void in the PLM software market. Another freelance company that offers tech-packs, but in Adobe Illustrator, is Just D-zine (Figure 7.4, pages 85–93).

Finding a program that is right for a particular company requires an analysis of that company's development process, production procedures, and distribution policies. Every bit of information must be broken down into pieces that are then used to set up each page of the package. Popular industry packages can also range from simple Microsoft Word or **Microsoft Excel** files to complex, point-of-sale packages. Many companies, such as Just D-zine, choose to build the tech-pack in Adobe or **Adobe Illustrator**.

Read now about Kiyomi Chansamone and her company, the hosting service TechPackCentral (Box 7.1).

BOX 7.1 Industry Insider Kiyomi Chansamone

TechPackCentral (TPC), a hosting service for Gerber Technology's WebPDM software, was founded in 2005 by Kiyomi Chansamone. Chansamone is a former senior implementation specialist for Gerber Technology and WebPDM administrator. Chansamone launched TPC to allow small- to medium-sized companies access to PDM software that was generally afforded only to larger apparel companies. TPC also maintains the high-end software for its clients, which include Baby Phat, Kellwood, and Hurley.

In addition to helping provide TPC services, Chansamone occasionally teaches Gerber career training classes.

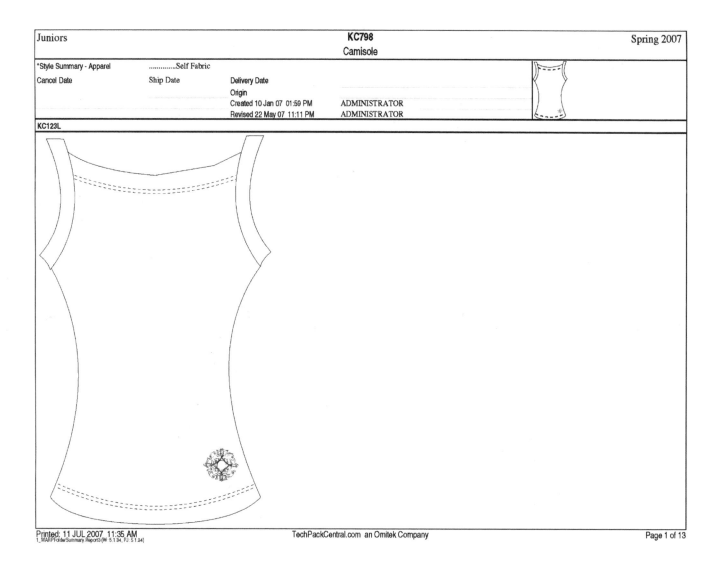

| Juniors | | | KC798 | | | Spring 2007 |
| | | | Camisole | | | |

*Style Summary - Apparel		..............Self Fabric			
Cancel Date	Ship Date	Delivery Date			
		Origin			
		Created 10 Jan 07 01:59 PM	ADMINISTRATOR		
		Revised 22 May 07 11:11 PM	ADMINISTRATOR		

KC123L

Figure 7.3a

Tech-pack by TechPackCentral,

using Gerber technology,

style summary/cover sheet

(page 1).

Juniors					KC798		Black	Pink	Red				Spring 2007

Juniors — **KC798** Camisole — Spring 2007

Cost Sheet	.............Self Fabric			
Cancel Date	Ship Date	Delivery Date		
		Origin		
		Created 10 Jan 07 11:04 PM	ADMINISTRATOR	
		Revised 08 Feb 07 10:29 PM	ADMINISTRATOR	

			Color: Combination:	Black	Pink	Red				
Item	**Item Information**	**Item Information Detail**	**Distribution**	1	1	1				
F0325 $3.25 FABRIC	UOM: YD			Black	Pink	Red				
Generic Fabric				0.5 YD	0.5 YD	0.5 YD				
				Sub For:						
Row Comments: Matte Jersey 96% Polyester/4% Spandex										
F0325 $3.25 FABRIC	UOM: YD			Black	Pink	White				
Generic Fabric				0.15 YD	0.15 YD	0.15 YD				
				Sub For:						
Row Comments: Matte Jersey 96% Polyester/4% Spandex										
TLBL0002 $.02 LABEL	UOM: EA			Pink	Pink	Pink				
Generic Trim				1 EA	1 EA	1 EA				
				Sub For:						
Row Comments: Main Label										
TLBL0003 $.03 LABEL	UOM: EA			Pink	Pink	Pink				
Generic Trim				1 EA	1 EA	1 EA				
				Sub For:						
Row Comments: Size/COO/CareLabel										
TLBL0002 $.02 LABEL	UOM: EA			White	White	White				
Generic Trim				1 EA	1 EA	1 EA				
				Sub For:						
Row Comments: UPC Label										

Figure 7.3b

Tech-pack by TechPackCentral, using Gerber technology, cost sheets (page 2).

Juniors		**KC798**	Spring 2007
		Camisole	

Fabric and Trim Images ....Self Fabric

Cancel Date	Ship Date	Delivery Date	
		Origin	
		Created 09 Feb 07 01:20 AM KCHANS01	
		Revised 09 Feb 07 01:20 AM KCHANS01	

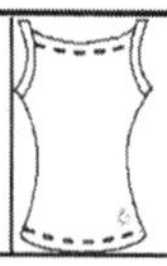

Vendor:		
Price:		
Color:		
Size/Width/Dimension:		
Comments:		

Figure 7.3c

Tech-pack by TechPackCentral,

using Gerber technology, trim

sheet (page 8).

Juniors				**KC798** Camisole						Spring 2007	

Measurement Specification Worksheet ....Self Fabric

Cancel Date	Ship Date	Delivery Date		
		Origin		
		Created 11 Jan 07 05:43 PM	ADMINISTRATOR	
		Revised 22 May 07 12:59 PM	ADMINISTRATOR	

Selected Range: XS, S, M, L, XL

P O M	Description	Tol (-)	Tol (+)	XS	[S]	M	L	XL			
A1	Across Top	-1/8	1/8	9 3/4	10	10 1/4	10 1/2	10 3/4			
A2	Chest - From Side Seam to Side Seam below binding Half	-1/4	1/4	12 1/2	13	13 1/2	14	14 1/2			
A3	Waist (10 inches from HPS)	-1/8	1/8	12 1/4	12 1/2	12 3/4	13	13 1/4			
A4	Sweep - From Side Seam to Side Seam Half Circumference	-1/4	1/4	14 1/2	15	15 1/2	16	16 1/2			
A5	Armhole Straight from the inside seam	-1/8	1/8	8 1/4	8 1/2	8 3/4	9	9 1/4			
A6	Length - From Top Seam to Bottom Seam	-1/4	1/4	20 1/2	21	21 1/2	22	22 1/2			

Figure 7.3d

Tech-pack by TechPackCentral, using Gerber technology, spec sheet (page 9).

Juniors			KC798						Spring 2007
			Camisole						

Fit Evaluation Worksheet ....Self Fabric

Cancel Date	Ship Date	Delivery Date				
		Origin				
		Created 12 Jan 07 01:35 AM	ADMINISTRATOR			
		Revised 22 May 07 12:59 PM	ADMINISTRATOR			

Company:	INCREMENTAL	Size Class:	Juniors	Pattern:	
Product Type:	Top	Factory:	None		
Agent Name:		Pattern Status:		Revision Status:	Revised
Sample Type:	1st Fit Sample	Date Sample Requested:		Sample Status:	
Date Received From		Vendor Measurer:	Sarah	Date Vendor Measured:	05 Jan 2007
Sample Measurer:	Kiyomi	Date Sample Measured:	12 Jan 2007	Fit Session Attendees:	

Selected Range: XS, S, M, L, XL

POM	Description	Eval Size S	Vendor Sample 1	Vendor Delta 1	Sample 1	Delta 1	Revised Spec	POM Comments
A1	Across Top	9 1/4	<9>	-1/4	<9>	-1/4		
A2	Chest - From Side Seam to Side Seam below binding	13 3/4	13 1/2	-1/4	<13>	-3/4	13	Vendor is 1/2" off
A3	Waist (10 inches from HPS)	12 1/2	<12 1/4>	-1/4	<12>	-1/2		Vendor is 1/4" off
A4	Sweep - From Side Seam to Side Seam Half	15	15	0	15	0		Ok
A5	Armhole Straight from the inside seam	8 1/2	8 1/2	0	<8>	-1/2		Vendor is 1/2" off
A6	Length - From Top Seam to Bottom Seam	21	21	0	21	0		Ok

Printed: 11 JUL 2007 11:35 AM
6_WAHPAMLrptMultiSampleEval2 (W 5 1.34, PJ 5.1.34)

TechPackCentral.com an Omitek Company

Page 10 of 13

Figure 7.3e

Tech-pack by TechPackCentral,
using Gerber technology,
quality assurance worksheet
(page 10).

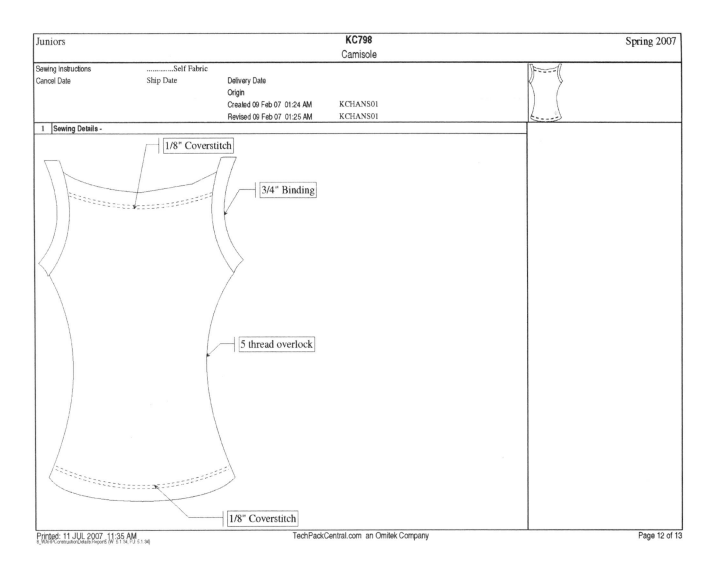

Figure 7.3f

Tech-pack by TechPackCentral,
using Gerber technology,
sewing instructions/
construction sheet (page 12).

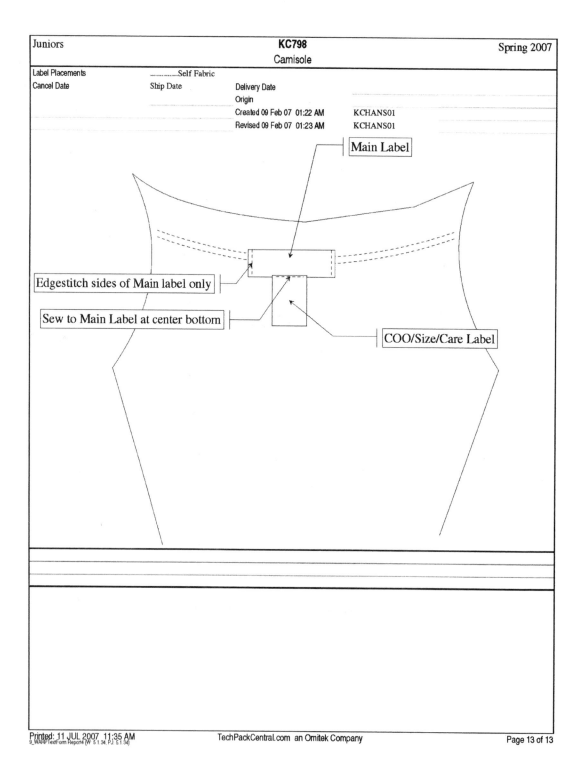

Juniors   **KC798**   Spring 2007
                                          Camisole

Label Placements   ....Self Fabric
Cancel Date   Ship Date   Delivery Date
                                               Origin
                                               Created 09 Feb 07 01:22 AM   KCHANS01
                                               Revised 09 Feb 07 01:23 AM   KCHANS01

Main Label

Edgestitch sides of Main label only

Sew to Main Label at center bottom

COO/Size/Care Label

Figure 7.3g

Tech-pack by
TechPackCentral, using
Gerber technology,
label sheet (page 13).

7.4a

COMBO	SELF	TRIM	RIB
1. Green Olive	PANTONE 17-0535	PANTONE 12-0738	PANTONE 17-0535 and PANTONE 12-0738
2. Teak	PANTONE 19-0617	PANTONE 12-0738	PANTONE 19-0617 and PANTONE 12-0738
3. Twilight Blue	PANTONE 19-3938	PANTONE 12-0738	PANTONE 19-3938 and PANTONE 12-0738

COMBO 1 Green Olive
COMBO 2 Teak
COMBO 3 Twilight Blue

7.4b

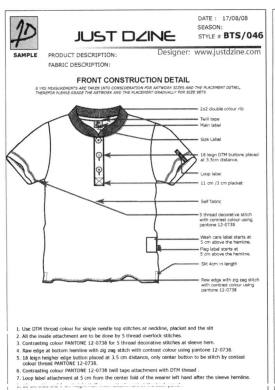

FRONT CONSTRUCTION DETAIL

8 YRS MEASUREMENTS ARE TAKEN INTO CONSIDERATION FOR ARTWORK SIZES AND THE PLACEMENT DETAIL, THEREFOR PLEASE GRADE THE ARTWORK AND THE PLACEMENT GRADUALLY FOR SIZE SETS.

- 2x2 double colour rib
- Twill tape
- Main label
- Size Label
- 18 leign DTM buttons placed at 3.5cm distance.
- Loop label
- 11 cm /3 cm placket
- Self fabric
- 5 thread decorative stitch with contrast colour using pantone 12-0738
- Wash care label starts at 5 cm above the hemline.
- Flag label starts at 5 cm above the hemline.
- Slit 4cm in length
- Raw edge with zig zag stitch with contrast colour using pantone 12-0738

1. Use DTM thread colour for single needle top stitches at neckline, placket and the slit
2. All the inside attachment are to be done by 5 thread overlock stitches.
3. Contrasting colour PANTONE 12-0738 for 5 thread decorative stitches at sleeve hem.
4. Raw edge at bottom hemline with zig zag stitch with contrast colour using pantone 12-0738.
5. 18 leign heigher edge button placed at 3.5 cm distance, only center button to be stitch by contast colour thread PANTONE 12-0738.
6. Contrasting colour PANTONE 12-0738 twill tape attachment with DTM thread.
7. Loop label attachment at 5 cm from the center fold of the wearer left hand after the sleeve hemline.

7.4c

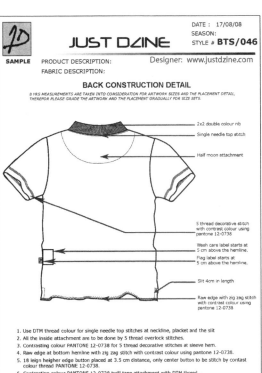

BACK CONSTRUCTION DETAIL

8 YRS MEASUREMENTS ARE TAKEN INTO CONSIDERATION FOR ARTWORK SIZES AND THE PLACEMENT DETAIL, THEREFOR PLEASE GRADE THE ARTWORK AND THE PLACEMENT GRADUALLY FOR SIZE SETS.

- 2x2 double colour rib
- Single needle top stitch
- Half moon attachment
- 5 thread decorative stitch with contrast colour using pantone 12-0738
- Wash care label starts at 5 cm above the hemline.
- Flag label starts at 5 cm above the hemline.
- Slit 4cm in length
- Raw edge with zig zag stitch with contrast colour using pantone 12-0738

1. Use DTM thread colour for single needle top stitches at neckline, placket and the slit
2. All the inside attachment are to be done by 5 thread overlock stitches.
3. Contrasting colour PANTONE 12-0738 for 5 thread decorative stitches at sleeve hem.
4. Raw edge at bottom hemline with zig zag stitch with contrast colour using pantone 12-0738.
5. 18 leign heigher edge button placed at 3.5 cm distance, only center button to be stitch by contast colour thread PANTONE 12-0738.
6. Contrasting colour PANTONE 12-0738 twill tape attachment with DTM thread .
7. Loop label attachment at 5 cm from the center fold of the wearer left hand after the sleeve hemline.
8. 18 cm wide and 9 cm height Half moon attachment at the back panel .

7.4d

Figure 7.4a–d

Tech-pack by Just D-zine: (a) cover sheet (page 1/12) (b) illustration sheet (page 2/12) (c) construction sheet, front detail (page 3/12) (d) construction sheet, back detail (page 4/12).

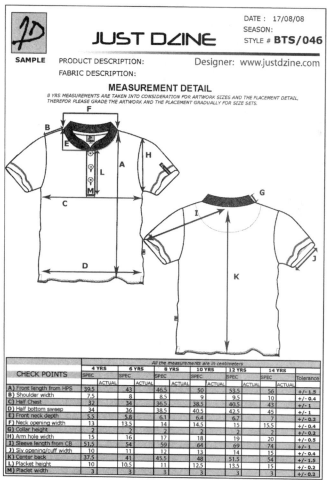

7.4e

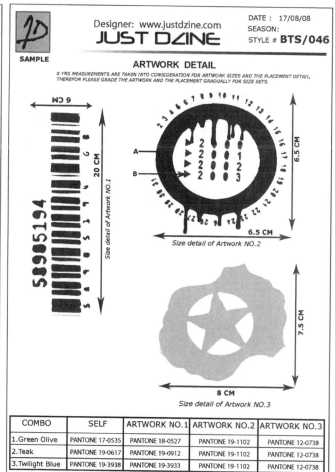

7.4f

Figure 7.4e–h

Tech-pack by Just D-zine:

(e) specification sheet

(page 5/12) (f) construction

detail sheet (page 6/12 (g)

construction detail sheet

(page 7/12) (h) construction

detail sheet (page 8/12).

Designer: www.justdzine.com
JUST DZINE

SAMPLE

DATE : 17/08/08
SEASON:
STYLE # **BTS/046**

ARTWORK NO 1. PLACEMENT AND DETAIL

8 YRS MEASUREMENTS ARE TAKEN INTO CONSIDERATION FOR ARTWORK SIZES AND THE PLACEMENT DETAIL, THEREFOR PLEASE GRADE THE ARTWORK AND THE PLACEMENT GRADUALLY FOR SIZE SETS.

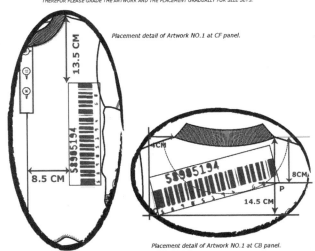

Placement detail of Artwork NO.1 at CF panel.

Placement detail of Artwork NO.1 at CB panel.

* PLEASE NOTE

1. ARTWORK NO.1 IS 6.5 CM IN HEIGHTS AND 6.5 CM IN WIDTH.

2. PLACEMENT OF THE ARTWORK NO.1 IS AT THE FRONT LEFT HAND SIDE BODICE AND IT SHOULD BE 13.5 CM BELOW HPS POINT AND 8.5 CM AWAY FROM THE CENTER FRONT LINE.

3. PLACEMENT OF THE ARTWORK NO.1 IS AT BACK PANEL AND IS CALCULATED WITH CETER POINT 'O' IT IS 14.5 CM BELOW AND 4 CM AWAY FROM HPS THE POINT 'P' IS 8 CM BELOW THE HPS.

4. ARTWORK NO.1 IS TONAL IN ALL THE THREE COMBOS PLEASE REFER THE PANTONE FOR ACCURACY

COMBO	SELF	ARTWORK COLOUR	ARTWORK SIZE
1.Green Olive	PANTONE 17-0535	PANTONE 18-0527	H 6 CM / W 20 CM
2.Teak	PANTONE 19-0617	PANTONE 19-0912	H 6 CM / W 20 CM
3.Twilight Blue	PANTONE 19-3938	PANTONE 19-3933	H 6 CM / W 20 CM

Artwork shown in the illustration is not the actual size please refer the measurement chart for accuracy

7.4g

Designer: www.justdzine.com
JUST DZINE

SAMPLE

DATE : 17/08/08
SEASON:
STYLE # **BTS/046**

ARTWORK NO 2. PLACEMENT AND DETAIL

8 YRS MEASUREMENTS ARE TAKEN INTO CONSIDERATION FOR ARTWORK SIZES AND THE PLACEMENT DETAIL, THEREFOR PLEASE GRADE THE ARTWORK AND THE PLACEMENT GRADUALLY FOR SIZE SETS.

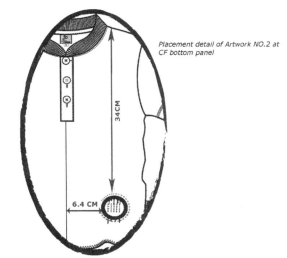

Placement detail of Artwork NO.2 at CF bottom panel

* PLEASE NOTE

1. ARTWORK NO.2 IS 6.5 CM IN HEIGHTS AND 6.5 CM IN WIDTH.

2. PLACEMENT OF THE ARTWORK NO 2. IS AT THE BOTTOM OF RIGHT HAND SIDE FRONT BODICE AND IT SHOULD BE 34 CM BELOW HPS POINT AND 6.4 CM FROM CF LINE.

3. ARTWORK NO.3 IS SAME (PANTONE 12-0738) IN ALL THE THREE COMBOS.

COMBO	SELF	ARTWORK COLOUR A	ARTWORK COLOUR B	ARTWORK SIZE
1.Green Olive	PANTONE 17-0535	PANTONE 19-1102	PANTONE 18-0527	H 6.5 CM / W 6.5 CM
2.Teak	PANTONE 19-0617	PANTONE 19-1102	PANTONE 19-0912	H 6.5 CM / W 6.5 CM
3.Twilight Blue	PANTONE 19-3989	PANTONE 19-1102	PANTONE 19-3933	H 6.5 CM / W 6.5 CM

Artwork shown in the illustration is not the actual size please refer the measurement chart for accuracy

7.4h

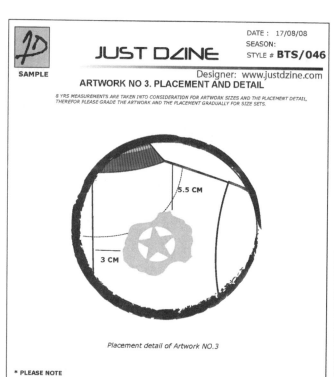

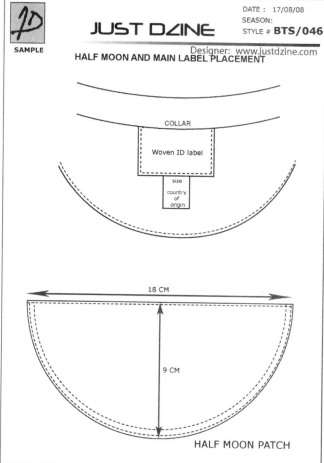

7.4i

7.4j

Figure 7.4i–l

Tech-pack by Just D-zine:
(i) construction detail sheet
(page 9/12) (j) construction/
label sheet (page 10/12) (k)
label/packaging sheet (page
11/12) (l) label packaging
sheet (page 12/12).

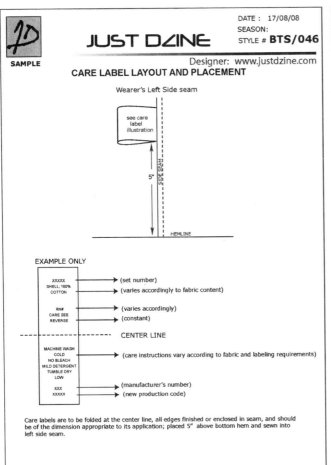

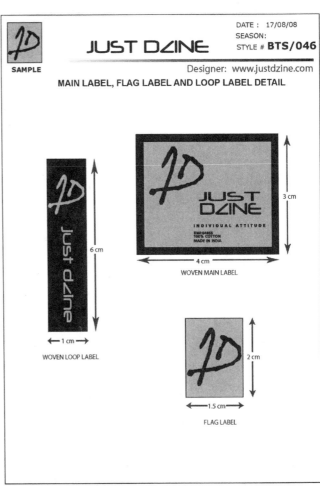

7.4k

7.4l

In the chapters that follow, you will be provided with a detailed breakdown of the production packages that have been prepared for this text. These have been provided as examples of what might be considered a good basic tech-pack. There is no one right way to construct a tech-pack; it is up to the production manager, designer, and company owner to decide what information should and should not be included.

The tech-pack templates for these chapters were created in Word, for illustrative purposes. However, for the templates that accompany the exercises at the end of each chapter, the popular Excel is used.

TECHNICAL PACKAGE LAB
Laboratory Applications

1. A technical package is used in the industry for what five purposes?

2. Julie and René own a 2-year-old nightshirt company in New York City. Annual revenue is already near $1 million. Because most of their merchandise is made in Turkey, René wonders if they should invest in a PLM or PDM system for the business; right now they use an Excel spreadsheet that he designed to track production and sales.
    a. Do you think they should continue using the spreadsheet René designed? Why or why not?
    b. Would Julie and René be better off investing in a PLM or a PDM system? Explain your answer.
    c. What other systems could Julie and René use to track production and sales?

REFERENCES

"Apparel Announces Its First Software Scorecard Results." Apparel Technology and Business Insight—From Concept to Consumer, May 1, 2006. http://www.apparelmag.com/ME2/Audiences/dirmod.asp?sid=&nm=&type=MultiPublishing&mod=Publis hingTitles&mid=CD746117C0BB4828857A1831CE707DBE&tier=4&id=8174906 FA53240E1811680E78739FC42&AudID=6E90D534423344039C0F44A6552F3927 (accessed June 3, 2009).

Centric Software. http://www.centricsoftware.com/aboutus/indux.asp?s=exec-team.

Corcoran, Cate T. "Tech Packs Go Electric," *WWDBusiness.com,* November 14, 2006. http://www.wwd.com/business-news/tech-paccks-go-electric-1038396.

Fasanella, Kathleen."What Is a Tech Pack?" *Fashion Incubator, Lessons from the Sustainable Factory Floor,* March 12, 2008. http://www.fashion-incubator.com/archive/what_is_a_ tech_pack/ (accessed June 1, 2009).

"Fashion Apparel." Lectra. http://www.lectra.com/en/fashion_apparel/index.html (accessed June 4, 2009).

Gerber Technology. http://www.gerbertechnology.com/default.asp?contentID=8.

Harder, Frances. *Fashion for Profit: A Professional's Complete Guide to Designing, Manufacturing, and Marketing a Successful Line.* 8th ed. Rolling Hills Estates, CA: Fashion Business Incorporated, 2008.

Just D-zine, http://www.techpackdesign.com/tp.htm. Lectra Fashion PLM. http://www.lectra.com/en/fashion_apparel/customer_testimonials.html.

PDM Fashion Industry Software. http://www.apparelsearch.com/software_pdm_ fashion.htm.

Sharp, Julia Ridgway, and Virginia Hencken Elsasser. *Introduction to AccuMark, Pattern Design, and Product Data Management.* New York: Fairchild Publications, 2007.

Style Source Inc. http://www.style-source.com/contact/index.asp.

TechPackCentral.com. http://www.techpackcentral.com/39thandBroadway. http://www.39thandbroadway.com/ode-techpack/ (accessed June 1, 2009).

The Design Sheet

8

THE DESIGN SHEET: OVERVIEW

The design sheet, also called a cover or lead sheet, offers the user a first visual of the garment. The **design sheet** is akin to the cover of a school report, providing a look at what is to come. Much of the information contained on the design sheet is repeated on the tech-pack sheets that follow, although this depends somewhat on personal preference; not all designers will show both a front and back view of the garment on the first sheet, for example. Regardless of the information included, designers may choose from three different methods of creating the garment images they will input (Figure 8.1, page 99):

- Hand sketch
- Digital illustration
- Digital photo

A basic design sheet consists of the following:

- Company name (some companies also include their address and their phone and fax numbers)
- Style or group number/name (or both)
- Season
- Garment label/brand (this is especially important if the company produces more than one line of products)
- Color information
- Sketch, digital illustration, or digital photo
- Approval boxes

OBJECTIVES

- Understand the purpose and uses of a basic design sheet.

- Identify the parts of a basic design sheet.

- Recognize industry design sheets created by commonly used software applications.

PREPARING A DESIGN SHEET

A detailed explanation of the parts of the design sheet follows, along with instructions for preparing one. A sample sheet is provided for your reference (Figure 8.2).

HEADING

Every sheet should have a heading. The example heading shows "Design Sheet"; most sheets will use "Design Sheet," "Cover Sheet," or "Lead Sheet." The page number is also shown in the heading. Page numbers are very important for keeping order in the tech-pack. Some companies simply number their pages in a running order, whereas others number them as part of the whole (e.g., "page 1 of 8"). Figure 8.2 uses the former method, Gerber Technology tech-packs, the latter.

COMPANY INFORMATION

Companies differ in how much information they provide on their sheets. Of all the components of the tech-pack, the design sheet should offer the most information about the company—company name, address, and phone and fax numbers. However, there is no one standard.

GARMENT INFORMATION

Some of the information listed in this section—group name, season, and garment label—defines the sheet as it is introduced into production. You will notice in future pages that this information transfers to the heading, as the focus shifts.

SEASON

This box lists the style's season. The season is especially valuable when keeping track of overlapping seasons and for basic styles that may repeat from season to season.

FABRIC INFORMATION

The fabric content and colorway are offered as a quick guide; a separate fabric sheet lists the information necessary for production.

SKETCH, DIGITAL ILLUSTRATION, OR DIGITAL PHOTO

The picture is the most important feature of this page, offering a quick reference to the entire pack. Some designers offer both a front and back view, some offer the front view only; some designers choose color, some choose black and white. A place may be provided for the designer's initials if assistants work on the tech-packs. This is a way for the head designer to sign off on, or approve, others' work. If a sketch is used, it needs to be scanned into the sheet. Digital photos and illustrations can be saved in a design file or created on or dropped directly onto the page.

APPROVAL BOXES

The boxes at the bottom of Figure 8.2 sheet are generally added to all tech-packs, although not necessarily at the bottom. The dates a pack is started, revised, and finally approved reveal at what stage in the production process the garment has advanced and are important for all parties involved to know.

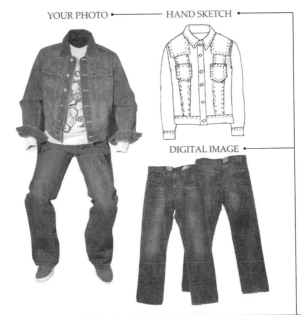

YOUR PHOTO · HAND SKETCH ·

DIGITAL IMAGE ·

Figure 8.1

Three methods of inputting images.

HEADING

COMPANY INFORMATION

SKETCH, DIGITAL ILLUSTRATION, OR DIGITAL PHOTO (at left)

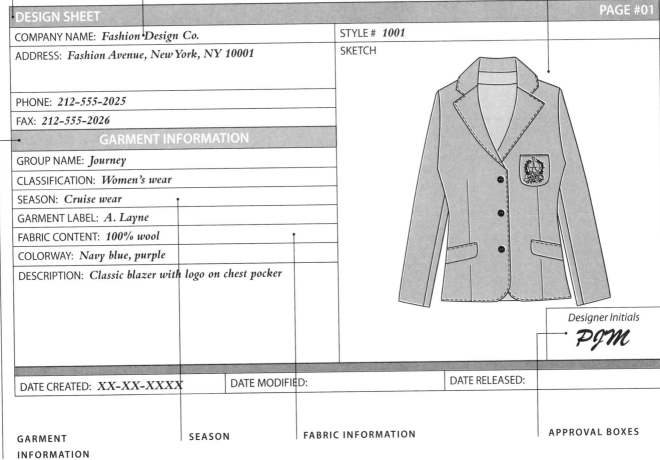

DESIGN SHEET	PAGE #01
COMPANY NAME: *Fashion Design Co.*	STYLE # *1001*
ADDRESS: *Fashion Avenue, New York, NY 10001*	SKETCH
PHONE: *212-555-2025*	
FAX: *212-555-2026*	
GARMENT INFORMATION	
GROUP NAME: *Journey*	
CLASSIFICATION: *Women's wear*	
SEASON: *Cruise wear*	
GARMENT LABEL: *A. Layne*	
FABRIC CONTENT: *100% wool*	
COLORWAY: *Navy blue, purple*	
DESCRIPTION: *Classic blazer with logo on chest pocker*	

Designer Initials
PJM

DATE CREATED: *XX-XX-XXXX*	DATE MODIFIED:	DATE RELEASED:

GARMENT INFORMATION

SEASON

FABRIC INFORMATION

APPROVAL BOXES

Figure 8.2

Sample design sheet.

INDUSTRY DESIGN SHEET

As discussed in Chapter 7, there are several different programs in which to build a technical package. For illustrative purposes, this text shows a package built in Word; however, in the industry, Excel files are commonly used. Figures 8.3 and 8.4 are further examples of typical tech-pack sheets. The first (Figure 8.3) is a Gerber tech-pack page, created by TechPackCentral. (Note that the heading on this sheet, "Style Summary–Apparel," does not conform with common practice; as stated previously, there is no right or wrong way to build a tech-pack.) The second image (Figure 8.4, next page) was created in Illustrator, a program popular with the many freelancers who are hired to design the images used in tech-packs. Here the image, by the artist and designer Jillian Krebsbach, has been dropped into an Excel spreadsheet to provide a grid for inserting the needed information.

Owing to the popularity of the tech-pack, a new crop of freelance designers, illustrators, and graphic artists has joined the fashion industry. Box 8.1 describes the path of one such designer, Teri Davis.

Figure 8.3

Gerber tech-pack page, created by TechPackCentral.

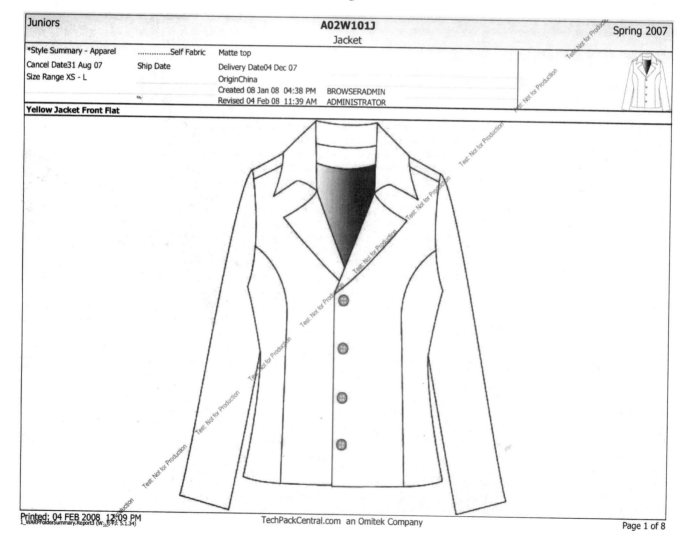

Juniors	A02W101J		Spring 2007
	Jacket		

*Style Summary – Apparel	............Self Fabric	Matte top	
Cancel Date31 Aug 07	Ship Date	Delivery Date04 Dec 07	
Size Range XS - L		OriginChina	
		Created 08 Jan 08 04:38 PM BROWSERADMIN	
		Revised 04 Feb 08 11:39 AM ADMINISTRATOR	

Yellow Jacket Front Flat

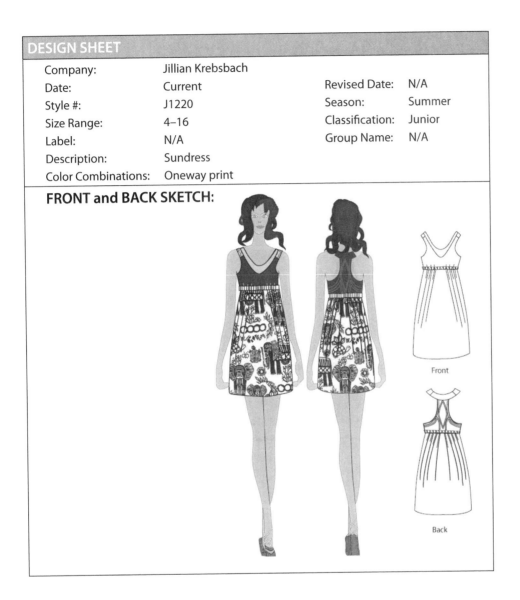

DESIGN SHEET

Company:	Jillian Krebsbach		
Date:	Current	Revised Date:	N/A
Style #:	J1220	Season:	Summer
Size Range:	4–16	Classification:	Junior
Label:	N/A	Group Name:	N/A
Description:	Sundress		
Color Combinations:	Oneway print		

FRONT and BACK SKETCH:

Front

Back

Figure 8.4

Jillian Krebsbach designed this image in Illustrator and then dropped it into an Excel file.

BOX 8.1   Industry Insider Teri Davis

For Teri Davis, becoming a designer was a natural outgrowth of her passion for the outdoors. Davis founded Confluence Design, a freelance design firm in Jackson, Wyoming, specializing in outerwear, activewear, and casual sportswear, after years of working in the sports apparel industry—first at Obermeyer, a skiwear company in Aspen, Colorado, and then at Columbia Sportswear, in Portland, Oregon. While at Columbia, Davis earned a degree in Apparel Design from the Art Institute. She also holds a BS in International Business and a BA in International Studies.

Confluence Design is at the confluence of the Hoback and Snake Rivers—hence its name. Davis, a skier, snowboarder, hiker, and mountain biker, finds inspiration from nature and the active lifestyle: "'I cannot count how many ideas have come from directly from hiking, biking, playing in the snow in a variety of ways—nor can I measure the inspiration that has come from being around so many other outdoor enthusiasts— watching what they wear and listening to what they want'" (Confluence Design).

DESIGN SHEET LAB
Laboratory Applications

1. Using the template provided (Figure 8.5), create a design sheet for a garment design of your own creation (your instructor may provide one for you instead). Fill in the information using this chapter's "Preparing a Design Sheet" section (pp. 98–99).

2. Design your own design sheet. What information do you believe should be added? What should be deleted?

3. Check the listings on at least two online job boards. How many ads can you find for tech-pack illustrators?

REFERENCES

Confluence Design. http://www.confluencedesigninc.com/index.cfm?id=profile (accessed June 1, 2009).

Encyclopedia Britannica Online. http://www.britannica.com/#tab=active~home%2C items~home&title=Britannica%20Online%20Encyclopedia.

"Using Illustration: What Every Client Needs to Know." Susan Bercu Design Studio. http://www.bercudesign.com/process/illustration.pdf (accessed October 13, 2009).

DESIGN SHEET		PAGE #01

COMPANY NAME:

ADDRESS:

PHONE:

FAX:

GARMENT INFORMATION

GROUP NAME:

CLASSIFICATION:

SEASON:

GARMENT LABEL:

FABRIC CONTENT:

COLORWAY:

DESCRIPTION:

STYLE #

SKETCH

Designer Initials

DATE CREATED:

DATE MODIFIED:

DATE RELEASED:

Figure 8.5

Design sheet template.

ILLUSTRATION SHEET: OVERVIEW

The illustration sheet looks very similar to the design sheet. It can be eliminated if designers or production managers choose to give a more in-depth version of a design sheet. The advantage of an **illustration sheet** is that it clarifies the **colorways**, or color scheme, of any given design. As mentioned previously, the designer may choose to forgo the illustration sheet, simply showing the colors in small images on the side of the page (see Figure 7.1, page 74). However, the designer may instead decide to color each garment and add an illustration page to the pack. An illustration sheet may also be used to show the front and back views of a garment if the designer has not done so on the design page.

Figure 9.1 (page 107) was prepared by Core Design Factory. Each item sketched was used for a tech-pack illustration sheet, even though the sketches are shown in only one colorway. The sheet shows three garments together as an output page, with a garment sketch as well. Core Design Factory would have also included a design sheet for each illustration, but only in front view.

A basic illustration sheet contains the following:

- **Company name (some companies also include their address and their phone and fax numbers)**
- **Style or group number/name (or both)**
- **Season**
- **Garment label/brand (this is especially important if the company produces more than one line of products)**
- **Color information**
- **Sketch, digital illustration, or digital photo**
- **Fabric information**
- **Fabric style number and width**
- **Size ranges**
- **Delivery dates**
- **Comments**
- **Approval boxes**

OBJECTIVES

- **Understand the purpose and uses of an illustration sheet.**

- **Identify the parts of a basic illustration sheet.**

- **Recognize an industry illustration sheet.**

PREPARING AN ILLUSTRATION SHEET

A detailed explanation of the parts of the illustration sheet follows, along with instructions for preparing one. A sample sheet is provided for your reference (Figure 9.2).

HEADING

Once again, every sheet should have a heading. Like the design sheet, the page number is shown in the heading; we are at page 2.

COMPANY INFORMATION

The company information is simply repeated from page 1. Many designers who post on blogs write that they find this time-consuming; however, if pages get separated from the pack, it is best to have this information, for identification purposes. Some of the larger companies who supply tech-pack software are trying to solve the problem of repeating input information.

GARMENT INFORMATION

Here the garment information is repeated, including group name, classification (women's wear, menswear, juniors, and so on), label, and colorway, under the main heading.

SKETCH BOX

The sketch, photo, or illustrated image is the most important feature of this sheet. The picture is offered to show the various colorways in which the garment is to be produced. A small box has again been added for the head designer's initials.

FABRIC INFORMATION

The last line of boxes on this sheet resembles those on the fabric sheet. This is a matter of choice; this information could have been placed above the sketches. (Again, there is no right or wrong way to set up a tech-pack sheet.) The fabric information provides a quick view of what is to come if the fabric sheets are not ready for production. At this point, style number of the fabric and its width are not that important, so the comment in that box tells the user that they will be provided on the fabric sheet.

SIZE RANGES

Size range information is also offered here. The design sheet was just the "cover" to the report; now it is time to get into the facts of garment production.

DELIVERY DATES

This example shows a garment early in the production process, so even though there is a delivery date box, a date is not set. A date should be set by the time the tech-pack is modified, as is noted in the next box: "Comments."

APPROVAL BOXES

Also added are boxes for the date the garment is created, the date it is modified, and the date it is released for production.

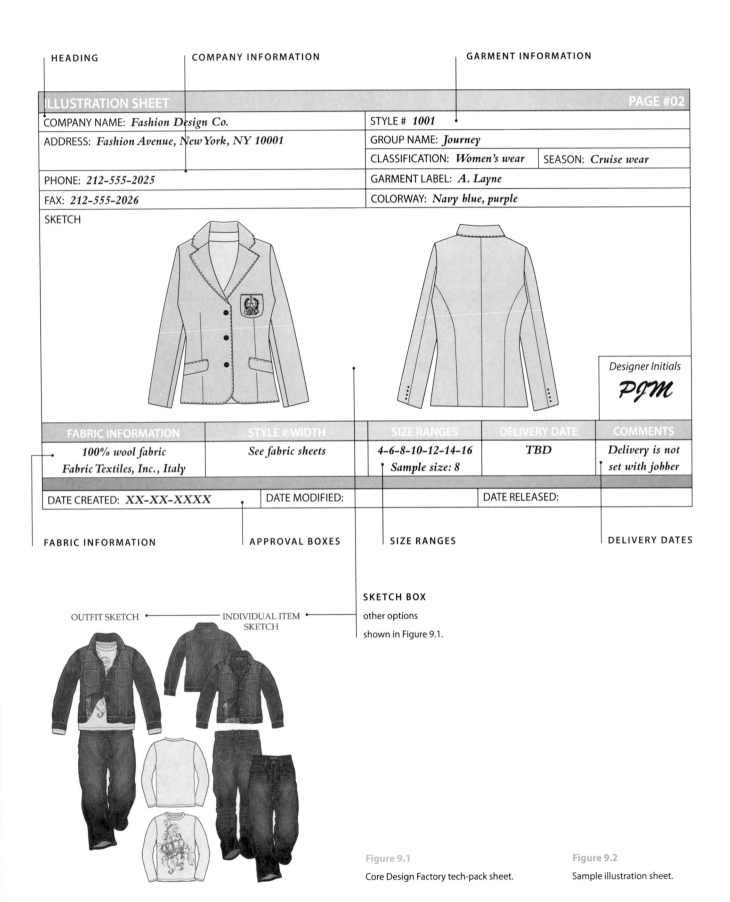

HEADING COMPANY INFORMATION GARMENT INFORMATION

ILLUSTRATION SHEET PAGE #02

COMPANY NAME: *Fashion Design Co.*

ADDRESS: *Fashion Avenue, New York, NY 10001*

PHONE: *212-555-2025*

FAX: *212-555-2026*

STYLE # *1001*

GROUP NAME: *Journey*

CLASSIFICATION: *Women's wear* | SEASON: *Cruise wear*

GARMENT LABEL: *A. Layne*

COLORWAY: *Navy blue, purple*

SKETCH

Designer Initials *PJM*

FABRIC INFORMATION	STYLE # WIDTH	SIZE RANGES	DELIVERY DATE	COMMENTS
100% wool fabric Fabric Textiles, Inc., Italy	*See fabric sheets*	*4-6-8-10-12-14-16 Sample size: 8*	*TBD*	*Delivery is not set with jobber*

DATE CREATED: *XX-XX-XXXX* | DATE MODIFIED: | | DATE RELEASED:

FABRIC INFORMATION APPROVAL BOXES SIZE RANGES DELIVERY DATES

SKETCH BOX
other options
shown in Figure 9.1.

OUTFIT SKETCH INDIVIDUAL ITEM SKETCH

Figure 9.1
Core Design Factory tech-pack sheet.

Figure 9.2
Sample illustration sheet.

INDUSTRY ILLUSTRATION SHEET

Not all companies and designers use an illustration sheet like the one in Figure 9.2. Figure 9.3 shows a Henley sketch, front and back views, colored three ways. The company name and color information are very prominent on this sheet, as well as the style number. This sheet does not give a lot of other information, as it is a sales sample for industry clients who may wish to contract with the firm Just D-zine.

As mentioned in Chapter 8, a new crop of freelance designers, illustrators, and graphic artists has joined the field of writing technical packages. Fashion merchandisers and textile designers are also part of this new group of professionals looking to work in the growing and lucrative field of tech packaging. Just D-zine, which was formed by a diverse group of industry professionals, is highlighted in Box 9.1.

BOX 9.1 Industry Insider Just D-zine

Just D-zine was formed in 2007 by a fashion designer, a graphic designer, a textile designer, an accessory designer, and a fashion merchandiser. The company they formed offers a variety of services, including the garment tech-pack, illustration, graphic design for prints and embroidery, presentation boards, visual merchandising, manufacturing, production, footwear, and bag and accessory design. Just D-zine clients include fashion houses, international brand owners, and retailers.

Just D-zine strives to achieve each client's vision and to reinforce brand image while maintaining respect for the client's cultural identity and ethical standards.

JUST DZINE

DATE : 17/08/08
SEASON:
STYLE # **BTS/046**

SAMPLE

PRODUCT DESCRIPTION:

FABRIC DESCRIPTION:

Designer: www.justdzine.com

COMBO 1
Green Olive

COMBO 2
Teak

COMBO 3
Twilight Blue

COMBO	SELF	TRIM	RIB
1.Green Olive	PANTONE 17-0535	PANTONE 12-0738	PANTONE 17-0535 and PANTONE 12-0738
2.Teak	PANTONE 19-0617	PANTONE 12-0738	PANTONE 19-0617 and PANTONE 12-0738
3.Twilight Blue	PANTONE 19-3938	PANTONE 12-0738	PANTONE 19-3938 and PANTONE 12-0738

Figure 9.3

Illustration sheet by

Just D-zine.

ILLUSTRATION SHEET LAB
Laboratory Applications

1. Using the template provided (Figure 9.4), create an illustration sheet for a garment design of your own creation (your instructor may provide one for you instead). Fill in the information using this chapter's "Preparing an Illustration Sheet" section (pp. 106–107).

2. Design you own illustration sheet. What information do you believe should be added? What should be deleted?

3. Adobe Illustrator is a very popular program with designers. If you have it, or access to it, sketch a few garments, then change the colors to show a few colorways. Can you add prints to your designs? Change the print colors.

REFERENCE

Just D-zine. http://www.techpackdesign.com/.

ILLUSTRATION SHEET		PAGE #02
COMPANY NAME:	STYLE #	
ADDRESS:	GROUP NAME:	
	CLASSIFICATION:	SEASON:
PHONE:	GARMENT LABEL:	
FAX:	COLORWAY:	

SKETCH

Designer Initials

FABRIC INFORMATION	STYLE WIDTH	SIZE RANGES	DELIVERY DATE	COMMENTS

DATE CREATED:	DATE MODIFIED:	DATE RELEASED:

Figure 9.4

Illustration sheet template.

The Fabric Sheet

FABRIC SHEET: OVERVIEW

The fabric sheet offers the user a visual of the garment's fabric. Much of the information contained in the design sheet is repeated in the **fabric sheet**, with the addition of an attached swatch of fabric or a fabric scan. If several colors are used, more fabric sheets can be generated. This visual is extremely important to manufacturers when similar fabric types are used in various garments within a vendor's line. Not all manufactures use a fabric sheet for every color; some put all their swatches on one page. This is again a question of preference.

A basic fabric sheet has the following elements:

- Company name (and occasionally its address and phone and fax numbers)
- Style or group number/name (or both)
- Season
- Fabric information (Table 10.1, page 116)
- Color information
- Garment label/brand
- Size range
- Delivery dates
- Sketch, digital illustration, or digital photo
- Fabric swatch or scan
- Approval boxes

PREPARING A FABRIC SHEET

Unlike the design sheet, which was broken into four distinct sections, the fabric sheet provided has six sections. They are labeled for illustrative purposes; generally, sections are not labeled, as section titles use up precious space. This is a basic fabric sheet; as with the other sheets discussed, fabric sheets vary by company (Figure 10.1, pages 114–115).

A detailed explanation of the parts of the fabric sheet follows, along with instructions for preparing one. A sample sheet is provided for your reference (Figure 10.1).

OBJECTIVES

- **Understand the purpose and uses of a basic fabric sheet.**

- **Identify the parts of a basic fabric sheet.**

- **Recognize an industry fabric sheet.**

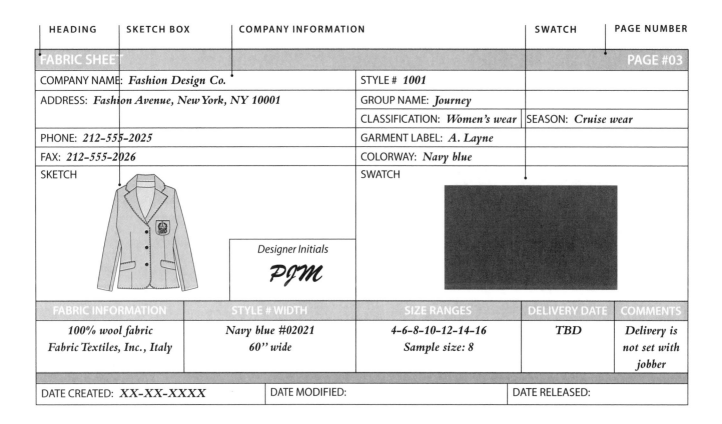

HEADING | SKETCH BOX | COMPANY INFORMATION | SWATCH | PAGE NUMBER

FABRIC SHEET | **PAGE #03**

COMPANY NAME: *Fashion Design Co.*	STYLE # *1001*	
ADDRESS: *Fashion Avenue, New York, NY 10001*	GROUP NAME: *Journey*	
	CLASSIFICATION: *Women's wear*	SEASON: *Cruise wear*
PHONE: *212-555-2025*	GARMENT LABEL: *A. Layne*	
FAX: *212-555-2026*	COLORWAY: *Navy blue*	

SKETCH

Designer Initials
PJM

SWATCH

FABRIC INFORMATION	**STYLE # WIDTH**	**SIZE RANGES**	**DELIVERY DATE**	**COMMENTS**
100% wool fabric *Fabric Textiles, Inc., Italy*	*Navy blue #02021* *60" wide*	*4-6-8-10-12-14-16* *Sample size: 8*	*TBD*	*Delivery is not set with jobber*

| DATE CREATED: *XX-XX-XXXX* | DATE MODIFIED: | DATE RELEASED: |

Figure 10.1a

Sample fabric sheet showing navy blue colorway.

HEADING
Just like every sheet, the fabric sheet needs a heading.

PAGE NUMBER
The page number becomes very important in this section. The first fabric sheet is numbered page 3. If, however, there are six colorways, pages 3 thru to 8 are added. In the sample provided, the navy blue colorway is on page 3, and the purple color is on page 4.

COMPANY INFORMATION
The company information is repeated as well as the group name, style number, and season. They are all included under the main heading, as the focus of this sheet is fabric.

FABRIC INFORMATION
The fabric information is repeated, but it is now moved to the bottom of the page, and more information is given than on the design and illustration sheets. Here, this section is used to verify the fabric information and to ensure that the correct fabric is cut for the corresponding style. **Fabrics**—cloth of any type made from woven, knitted, or felted thread or fibers—are generally the most expensive components of a garment; therefore, the information in this section is essential for preventing a fabric mistake from happening further along in the production process. In addition, the sketch and fabric scan or swatch gives the user a visual reference (in this example, of wool). The style number of the fabric and the width of the cloth are also listed on this sheet. Finally, as stated above, each color receives its own sheet—even if a style is offered in a dozen or more colors.

SKETCH, DIGITAL ILLUSTRATION, OR DIGITAL PHOTO

The picture or photo is repeated to offer a quick reference to the user, but the size is reduced to make room for the fabric swatch or scan. Because fabric information is paramount on this sheet, the sketch is moved to the left side. A place is still provided for the designer's initials, if needed.

SWATCH

A small section is provided for the colorway (in this case, the first color used) and for the color name. Again, more pages are added for additional color numbers and names. A large section is provided for the swatch or fabric scan. In most cases, a swatch is attached to the first fabric sheet, and a digital scan is added to the file for all other copies. This saves time and money and reduces the likelihood of a swatch falling off the page.

SIZE RANGES

Size range information is again listed.

DELIVERY DATES

The delivery date is still not set, but the box is shown on this sheet as well, with a corresponding note in the comments box.

APPROVAL BOXES

Also added are the approval boxes: the date the garment is created, the date it is modified, and the date it is released for production.

Figure 10.1b

Sample fabric sheet showing purple colorway.

FABRIC SHEET				PAGE #04
COMPANY NAME: *Fashion Design Co.*		STYLE # *1001*		
ADDRESS: *Fashion Avenue, New York, NY 10001*		GROUP NAME: *Journey*		
		CLASSIFICATION: *Women's wear*	SEASON: *Cruise wear*	
PHONE: *212-555-2025*		GARMENT LABEL: *A. Layne*		
FAX: *212-555-2026*		COLORWAY: *Purple*		
SKETCH	Designer Initials *PJM*	SWATCH		

FABRIC INFORMATION	STYLE # WIDTH	SIZE RANGES	DELIVERY DATE	COMMENTS
100% wool fabric *Fabric Textiles, Inc., Italy*	*Purple #03021* *60" wide*	*4-6-8-10-12-14-16* *Sample size: 8*	*TBD*	*Delivery is not set with jobber*

DATE CREATED: *XX-XX-XXXX*	DATE MODIFIED:		DATE RELEASED:	

FABRIC INFORMATION   APPROVAL BOXES   SIZE RANGES   DELIVERY DATES

INDUSTRY FABRIC SHEET

Chapter 8 presented a tech-page created by Jillian Krebsbach in Illustrator and dropped into an Excel spreadsheet. Another example of her work is shown in Figure 10.2. This time, Jillian has provided a fabric sheet; note how different her sheet is from the one in Figure 10.1. Jillian's sheet is similar in form to those of a company at which she was once employed. It is a common practice for designers to get used to a style, borrowing the parts they like and incorporating them into their own packages. This is one reason why there are so many different packages out there today. Let's learn a little more about the designer Jillian Krebsbach (Box 10.1).

TABLE 10.1   Textile Fibers for the Apparel Industry

Abaca	Glass fiber	Pina	Ramie
Acetate	Hemp	Polyactide	Rayon
Acrylate	Jute	Polyester	Silk
Acrylic	Kenaf	Polyolefin	Sisal
Alginate	Kevlar	Polypropylene	Sorona polymer
Alpaca	Linen	Polyurethane	Soybean protein
Aramid	Lurex	POY	fiber
Bamboo	Lycra		Spandex
Basalt	Lyocell		Tencel
Carbon	Mohair		Vicuna
Cashmere	Modacrylic		Viscose
Coir (coconut fiber)	Model		Wool
Cotton	Nylon		
Flax	Olefin		

Adapted from "Textile Fiber" Freebase. http://www.freebase.com/view/base/textiles/views/textile_fiber (accessed June 29, 2009).

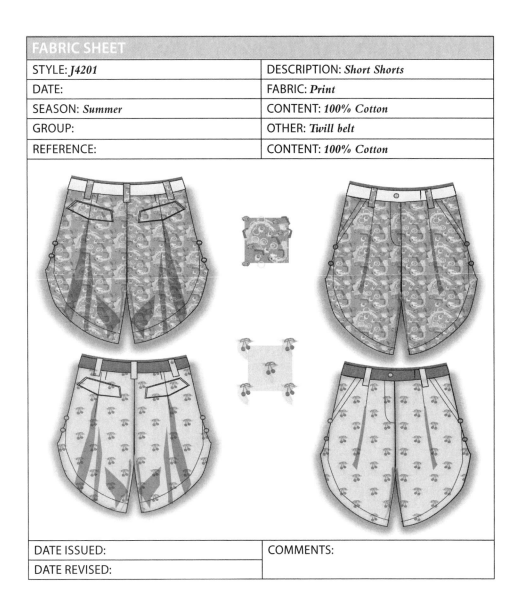

FABRIC SHEET	
STYLE: *J4201*	DESCRIPTION: *Short Shorts*
DATE:	FABRIC: *Print*
SEASON: *Summer*	CONTENT: *100% Cotton*
GROUP:	OTHER: *Twill belt*
REFERENCE:	CONTENT: *100% Cotton*

DATE ISSUED:	COMMENTS:
DATE REVISED:	

Figure 10.2

Fabric sheet from the portfolio of Jillian Krebsbach.

BOX 10.1 Industry Insider Jillian Krebsbach

The designer Jillian Krebsbach is just beginning her career in the fashion industry, but already she has ambitious plans for her future. Krebsbach, who currently works for the Macy's Merchandising Group in its private label children's wear tech design department, hopes soon to launch, with a friend, a line of luxury women's running wear. Previously, Krebsbach was an assistant technical designer for the Worth Collection.

Krebsbach's designs have been featured in *Threads* magazine, the FGI Dallas Career Day Apparel Mart, and the Banneker Academy fashion show fundraiser held in Brooklyn, New York, in 2009. Krebsbach knows many of the popular software programs required in the industry today: Lectra Modaris, Adobe Illustrator, and Corel DESIGNER. Krebsbach holds a bachelor's degree in Fashion Design from Baylor University in Waco, Texas, and a Certificate in Draping from the Fashion Institute of Technology in New York.

FABRIC SHEET LAB

Laboratory Applications

1. Using the template provided (Figure 10.3), create a fabric sheet for a design of your own creation (your instructor may provide one for you instead). Fill in the information using this chapter's "Preparing a Fabric Sheet" section (pp. 113–115), and add a swatch of fabric or a scan in the swatch section. Make up several sheets, using different colors.

2. Design you own fabric sheet. What information do you believe should be added? What should be deleted?

3. Visit your local fabric store. From the end of the bolt, record the fabric resource (supplier), fabric content, and color name or number for at least six fabrics. Some fabrics—especially those offered in coordinating prints or stripes—may also have a group name, which you should record as well. How many different suppliers can you find?

REFERENCE

Krebsbach, Jillian. StylePortfolios.com. http://www.styleportfolios.com/portfolio.php?username=jilliankrebsbach.

FABRIC SHEET				PAGE #03
COMPANY NAME:		STYLE #		
ADDRESS:		GROUP NAME:		
		CLASSIFICATION:		SEASON:
PHONE:		GARMENT LABEL:		
FAX:		COLORWAY:		
SKETCH		SWATCH		

Designer Initials

FABRIC INFORMATION	STYLE WIDTH	SIZE RANGES	DELIVERY DATE	COMMENTS

DATE CREATED:	DATE MODIFIED:	DATE RELEASED:

Figure 10.3

Fabric sheet template.

COMPONENT SHEET: OVERVIEW

The **component sheet** lists every component, or constituent part, of the garment. Can you think of the items that go into a garment's construction? There are generally the body fabric; trim or interfacing fabrics, or both; fasteners; and thread. The component sheet is a detailed listing of these parts.

A component sheet consists of the following:

- **Company name (and occasionally its address and phone and fax numbers)**
- **Style or group number/name (or both)**
- **Season**
- **List of items, by vendor, code, and origin**
- **List of fabric content, by item**
- **List of the size, quantity, and unit of measure for each item**
- **List of the location of each item**
- **List of the colorways of each item**
- **Comments**
- **Approval boxes**

PREPARING A COMPONENT SHEET

A detailed explanation of the parts of the component sheet follows, along with instructions for preparing one. A sample sheet is provided for your reference (Figure 11.1).

HEADING
Just like the other sheets, every component sheet should have a heading. The sample shown in Figure 11.1 repeats the company name, group name, classification, basic fabric information, season, and style number. Again, the sheet offers a reference should the pages of the package be separated.

PAGE NUMBER
The page number continues to be important in this section. The fabric sheet ended on page 4 (see Figure 10.1, pages 114–115); the component sheet picks up where that sheet left off, with pages 5 and 6. However, if the components for

each color did not fit on one page, or if there were more than one colorway, then additional pages would be needed. Tech-packs can actually grow to be very large, depending on the amount of information provided and the number of colorways offered, making page numbering essential.

COMPONENT CHART

A chart of the garment components takes up the bulk of this sheet. The chart includes the following:

- *Item–Vendor–Code–Origin*—This column lists each item, the vendor or manufacturer of that item, a code or style number, and the item's country of origin (required by **U.S. labeling laws**).
- *Content*—The fabric or material content of each item is listed in this column. Fabric content is very important for several reasons: (1) A particular style might be made in both a natural and a blended fiber, making fabric identification imperative; (2) U.S. labeling laws require it; (3) the content offers the user a visual reference—wool versus cotton, for example.
- *Size–Quantity–Unit of Measure*—This column may have many different headings; some sheets will say "style" or "width" instead of size. No matter what heading is used, the column information is the same: the component fabric width, the component style, or the component size. The sample sheet in Figure 11.1 actually lists all three: a fabric width, a button size, and a shoulder pad style. Also listed are the quantity of each component as needed per garment and the unit of measure. For example, 1.58 yards (the quantity and unit of measure) of fabric are needed to make the sample blazer as well as a total of 11 of a gross (the quantity and unit of measure) of buttons. (Note: 1 gross equals 144.)
- *Location*—This column provides the location of a particular component. Not only is this a good visual reference, but it can also help eliminate mistaking one component for another and mixing up their placement.
- *Colorway*—The color of each component is given here. When a particular style has several more than one colorway, a corresponding component sheet will be generated for each. For example, in Figure 10.1 one page was generated for the navy blue version of the blazer and another sheet for the purple version of this style.
- *Comments*—A comment column lists any additional information. In some instances, images can be loaded into this column for further referencing. Or, let us say, for example, natural-colored interfacing was requested in the colorway column, but the purchasing agent knows that stock is low and that the new shipment may not arrive in time; he or she may comment, in this section, that white interfacing may be used as a substitute.

APPROVAL BOXES

These boxes are again added for signing off on the significant production dates.

The cover sheet was broken into four distinct sections, and the fabric sheet into five, but this sheet has only three. So much needs to be conveyed about the components that much of the other pertinent information is eliminated.

ITEM-VENDOR-CODE-ORIGIN   LOCATION   COLORWAY

COMPONENT SHEET		PAGE #05
COMPANY NAME: *Fashion Design Co.*	STYLE # *1001*	
ADDRESS: *Fashion Avenue, New York, NY 10001*	GROUP NAME: *Journey*	
	CLASSIFICATION: *Women's wear*	SEASON: *Cruise wear*
PHONE: *212–555–2025*	FABRIC CONTENT: *100% wool*	
FAX: *212–555–2026*	COLORWAY: *Navy blue*	

ITEM-VENDOR-CODE-ORIGIN	CONTENT	SIZE-QUANTITY-UNIT OF MEASURE	LOCATION	COLOR	COMMENTS
Lining *Just Linings, style #6620* *China*	*100% poly lining*	*45" wide, 1⅓ yard, per garment*	*Inside garment body, sleeves, and pockets*	*Navy #347*	*Any navy blue may be used for sample*
Interfacing *Pellon (factory stock)* *USA*	*80% poly / 20% nylon*	*22" wide, ⅓ yard*	*Collar / facing / cuffs*	*Beige*	*May substitute white in samples*
Buttons *D & G Co., style #14240* *Hong Kong*	*Brass*	*3, 25 ligne / gross, per garment*	*Center front*	*Sailor-Brass*	
Buttons *D & G Co., style #14240* *Hong Kong*	*Brass*	*8, 20 ligne / gross, per garment*	*On sleeve plackets*	*Sailor-Brass*	
Embroidered patch *EPM Co.* *USA*	*100% poly*	*1, 3" patch / gross, per garment*	*Chest pocket*	*Made to order / 4 color*	*Designer logo*
Shoulder pad *Austin Inc., style #3B* *China*	*50% cotton / 50% poly*	*Medium 2/gross pair, per garment*	*Shoulder seams*	*White*	
Thread *YAK Industries (factory stock)* *Malaysia*	*100% poly*	*Spool 5000, as needed per garment*	*All seams and hems*	*Navy #0215*	*May substitute if needed*

DATE CREATED: *XX-XX-XXXX*	DATE MODIFIED:	DATE RELEASED:

CONTENT   SIZE-QUANTITY-UNIT OF MEASURE   COMMENTS

Figure 11.1a

Sample component sheet showing navy blue colorway.

COMPONENT SHEET				PAGE #06	
COMPANY NAME: *Fashion Design Co.*			STYLE # *1001*		
ADDRESS: *Fashion Avenue, New York, NY 10001*			GROUP NAME: *Journey*		
			CLASSIFICATION: *Women's wear*		SEASON: *Cruise wear*
PHONE: *212-555-2025*			FABRIC CONTENT: *100% wool*		
FAX: *212-555-2026*			COLORWAY: *Purple*		
ITEM-VENDOR-CODE-ORIGIN	CONTENT	SIZE-QUANTITY-UNIT OF MEASURE	LOCATION	COLOR	COMMENTS
Lining *Just Linings, style #6620* *China*	*100% poly lining*	*45" wide, 1¹/₃ yard, per garment*	*Inside garment body, sleeves, and pockets*	*Purple #163*	*Any navy blue may be used for sample*
Interfacing *Pellon (factory stock)* *USA*	*80% poly/ 20% nylon*	*22" wide, ¹/₃ yard*	*Collar/facing/cuffs*	*Beige*	*May substitute white in samples*
Buttons *D & G Co., style #14240* *Hong Kong*	*Brass*	*3, 25 ligne/gross, per garment*	*Center front*	*Sailor-Brass*	
Buttons *D & G Co., style #14240* *Hong Kong*	*Brass*	*8, 20 ligne/gross, per garment*	*On sleeve plackets*	*Sailor-Brass*	
Embroidered patch *EPM Co.* *USA*	*100% poly*	*1, 3" patch/gross, per garment*	*Chest pocket*	*Made to order/4 color*	*Designer logo*
Shoulder pad *Austin Inc., style #3B* *China*	*50% cotton/ 50% poly*	*Medium 2/gross pair, per garment*	*Shoulder seams*	*White*	
Thread *YAK Industries (factory stock)* *Malaysia*	*100% poly*	*Spool 5000, as needed per garment*	*All seams and hems*	*Purple #2192*	*May substitute if needed*
DATE CREATED: *XX-XX-XXXX*		DATE MODIFIED:		DATE RELEASED:	

INDUSTRY COMPONENT SHEET

The tech-page in Figure 11.2 is titled "Trim Sheet," and although different in appearance, it is actually similar to the component sheet in Figure 11.1. The description column in this figure is a more detailed version of the item column in Figure 11.1, minus the rest of the vendor information, which has been moved to the mill column. Lot/style number gets its own column. Both sheets have content and location columns, but the sheet in Figure 11.2 uses "Placement" for "Location." Moreover, this sheet lists width instead of size, quantity, and unit of measure, and it does not have a comments column. Which sheet is better for production? Is one better than the other? It is really a matter of personal preference.

One of the reasons that manufacturers and retailers hire freelance designers to work on their tech-packs is flexibility. The cost for of a $100,000 software system can be prohibitive for a small manufacturer, not to mention the large monthly fees required by many of the service companies. These small manufacturers often rely on freelance designers who are not part of the company's full-time staff to create tech-pack illustrations that are imaginative and unique. Let us take a look at another of these talented designers (Box 11.1).

TRIM SHEET	GENERAL INFORMATION				
STYLE #: *S091426*					
BODY #: *D1406*	DESCRIPTION: *Paper-bag-waist dress; solid picot with self-color topstitching*			DATE CREATED:	
LABEL: *Designer Collection*	SIZE RANGE: *0-2-4-6-8-10-12-14-16-18-20*			DATE REVISED:	
				PATTERNMAKER:	
	MFG LOCATION:			DESIGN TECH:	
SEASON: *Spring 09*	LINE PLANE PG #: *40*				

DESIGN DETAILS: TRIM					
DESCRIPTION	LOT/STYLE #	MILL	CONTENT	PLACEMENT	WIDTH
Topstitching pp 404; be sure to use matching color; test thread and fabric for bleeding	*Heavy topstitching thread*	*Hong Kong/ Paris thread (coat is too expensive)*		*For pick stitch ★*	
★ Pick-stitching machine	*Pick stitching*			*All details*	
Zipper	*Stock*	*Mill stock*		*Center back*	
Lingerie straps	*Lingerie straps*	*HK*		*Inside shoulder seams*	
DATE PRINTED:		TIME PRINTED:			PAGE 2 OF 4

Figure 11.2 Trim sheet.

BOX 11.1 Industry Insider Zoë Anderson

In 2006 Zoë Anderson established ZLA Design, a freelance company offering Web site, graphic, and textile design. Anderson's client list is long and includes Laundry Studio, for which she created graphic patterns for the 2007 Textile Trade Show in Paris. Anderson has a passion for design and textiles and hopes eventually to start her own textile design business.

Previously, Anderson worked at Burlen, where she designed screen prints and repeats for underwear. While at Burlen, Anderson learned how to do technical drawings using Adobe Illustrator. Earlier, as a data entry clerk at a law firm, she was encouraged to learn Flash, as well as Photoshop and other design software, in order to design the company Web site. Anderson received a BA in Art from Smith College in 1994.

COMPONENT SHEET LAB
Laboratory Applications

1. Continue the process started in Chapter 7, using the template provided (Figure 11.3) to create a component sheet.

2. Design your own component sheet. What information do you believe should be added? What should be deleted?

3. Do research on the Internet, or use trade publications, to compile a list of component suppliers. How many can you find? Your instructor may assign a component type to each student or to groups of students for this assignment.

REFERENCES

"U.S. Labeling Laws You Need to Know about When Selling Your Handcrafted Apparel Items." http://www.about.com/ About.com. http://crochet.about.com/library/bllabel_apparel.htm (accessed July 7, 2009).

ZLA Design. http://zladesign.com/html/textile_design.html (accessed July 7, 2009).

COMPONENT SHEET						PAGE #04
COMPANY NAME:			STYLE #			
ADDRESS:			GROUP NAME:			
			CLASSIFICATION:		SEASON:	
PHONE:			FABRIC CONTENT:			
FAX:			COLORWAY:			

ITEM-VENDOR-CODE-ORIGIN	CONTENT	SIZE-QUANTITY-UNIT OF MEASURE	LOCATION	COLOR	COMMENTS

DATE CREATED:	DATE MODIFIED:	DATE RELEASED:

Figure 11.3

Component sheet template.

LABEL/PACKING SHEET: OVERVIEW

A **label/packing sheet** lists the instructions for labels, hangtags, and packing. You will see in the examples that follow that there are two distinct approaches to creating these sheets. In addition, manufacturers and retailers vary greatly in their packing processes. Most venders will comply with a retailer's request for **hangtags** (merchandise tags that provide pertinent information) and **bar coding** (labeling merchandise with an identifying computer code), but some retailers prefer to tag at their warehouse facilities. The same is true for packing. Many retailers, especially high-end, prefer special packing for their garments—extra tissue or fancy hangers. If this cannot be achieved at the vendor's plant, then the garment will be repacked at the warehouse. These instructions must all be listed on the label/packing sheet.

A label/packing sheet is composed of the following:

- Company name (and occasionally its address and phone and fax numbers)
- Style or group number/name (or both)
- Season
- List of items by vendor, code, and origin
- List of fabric content, by item
- List of the size, quantity, and unit of measure for each item
- List of the location of each item
- List of the colorways of each item
- Comments
- Approval boxes

PREPARING A LABEL/PACKING SHEET

The label/packing sheet is designed like the component sheet. A detailed explanation of the parts of the label/component sheet follows, along with instructions for preparing one. A sample is provided for your reference (Figure 12.1).

HEADING

The sample shown in Figure 12.1 repeats the company name, group name, classification, basic fabric information, season, and style number.

OBJECTIVES

- Understand the purpose and uses of a label/packing sheet.

- Identify the parts of a basic label/packing sheet.

- Recognize an industry label/packing sheet.

ITEM-VENDOR-CODE-ORIGIN   SIZE-QUANTITY-UNIT OF MEASURE   LOCATION   COLORWAY PAGE NUMBER

LABEL/PACKING SHEET

PAGE #07

COMPANY NAME: *Fashion Design Co.*		STYLE # *1001*	
ADDRESS: *Fashion Avenue, New York, NY 10001*		GROUP NAME: *Journey*	
		CLASSIFICATION: *Women's wear*	SEASON: *Cruise wear*
PHONE: *212–555–2025*		FABRIC CONTENT: *100% wool*	
FAX: *212–555–2026*		COLORWAY:	

ITEM-VENDOR-CODE-ORIGIN	CONTENT	SIZE-QUANTITY-UNIT OF MEASURE	LOCATION	COLOR	COMMENTS
Designer label *High Tech Label Co.* *Los Angeles, CA*	*100% poly*	*1 per garment* *Gross measure*	*Center back neck,* *on facing*	*3 color*	*Pull from stock*
Size tab *Print–Avery Dennison machine*	*100% poly*	*1 per garment*	*Center back neck,* *under designer* *label; right of care* *label*	*1 color*	*Print to fill order*
Care label *Print–Avery Dennison machine*	*100% poly*	*1 per garment*	*Center back neck,* *under designer* *label; left of size* *tab*	*1 color*	*Dry clean only* *Print to fill order*
Bar-code tag *Perfect China Supplies Ltd,* *Kowloon, Hong Kong*	*Transparent* *paper*	*1 per garment*	*Attach by Den-* *nison gun to* *sleeve cuff*	*2 color*	*Order by size range,* *color, and style* *number*
Hangtag *Perfect China Supplies Ltd,* *Kowloon, Hong Kong*	*Cardboard* *laminate*	*1 per garment*	*Attach by Den-* *nison gun to* *sleeve cuff*	*3 color*	*Pull from stock*

DATE CREATED: *XX-XX-XXXX*		DATE MODIFIED:		DATE RELEASED:

CONTENT   COMMENTS

Figure 12.1a

Sample label/packing sheet.

PAGE NUMBER

This text example requires two pages because there is too much information for a one-page sheet. However, if the fictitious manufacturer was to tag its garments at the warehouse, some of the notations could be eliminated, thus reducing the length to a single page.

LABEL/PACKING CHART

This sheet has a chart similar to that of the component sheet, but this one is for the information that will be necessary for labeling or packing the garment. Again, the chart takes up the bulk of the sheet and comprises these components:

- *Item–Vendor–Code–Origin*—This column lists each item, the vendor or manufacturer of that item, a code or style number, and the item's country of origin (good for referencing or reordering).
- *Content*—Here, content is simply listed as a reference for everyone working on the order.

LABEL/PACKING SHEET						PAGE #08
COMPANY NAME: *Fashion Design Co.*			STYLE # *1001*			
ADDRESS: *Fashion Avenue, New York, NY 10001*			GROUP NAME: *Journey*			
			CLASSIFICATION: *Women's wear*		SEASON: *Cruise wear*	
PHONE: *212-555-2025*			FABRIC CONTENT: *100% wool*			
FAX: *212-555-2026*			COLORWAY:			

ITEM-VENDOR-CODE-ORIGIN	CONTENT	SIZE-QUANTITY-UNIT OF MEASURE	LOCATION	COLOR	COMMENTS
Hangers #HD666020 *Hangersdirect.com*	*Plastic*	*1 per garment* *Gross measure*		*Clear*	*Pull from stock*
Size marker for hanger *Hangersdirect.com*	*Paper sticker*	*1 per garment* *500 per size/roll*	*On center* *top hanger*	*Each size* *is colored* *accordingly*	*Be sure to match up* *appropriately colored* *size sticker on hanger* *with garmentr*
Poly bags *NU-Era Wholesale* *St. Louis, MO*	*Plastic*	*1 per garment* *1000/roll*	*Over garment on* *hanger*	*Clear*	*Pull from stock*

DATE CREATED: *XX-XX-XXXX*	DATE MODIFIED:	DATE RELEASED:

- *Size–Quantity–Unit of Measure*—This column lets the user know how many items are needed per garment and how the items are packaged. (Note: 1 gross equals 144.)
- *Location*—Again, the location of each item is listed for the item to ensure correct placement on or over (polybag) the garment
- *Colorway*—The color of each item is listed here. This information can be important if a manufacturer or retailer owns several labels. A more specific comment can also be added for clarity.
- *Comments*—The comments column is for any additional information. In many cases, manufacturers stock common items and simply have vendors pull them from stock. A purchasing agent keeps track of inventory and refills as needed. These instructions would appear here. A scan of an item can also be added to this column.

Figure 12.1b

Sample label/packing sheet.

APPROVAL BOXES

Once again, boxes are added to the tech-sheet for approval dates.

Like the component sheet, this sheet only has three major sections. The large amount of information to be conveyed about the labeling and packing necessitates that most other information be eliminated.

INDUSTRY LABEL/PACKING SHEET

Figure 12.2 (next page) is a label sheet created by TechPackCentral that is very different from Figure 12.1. Unlike the chart in that figure, here we have an illustration of the garment in which the label placement is drawn. The sheet is simply titled "Label Placement." The rest of this client's pack is shown in Chapter 7 (see Figure 7.3). The client, TechPackCentral, used its cost sheet for much of the tech-pack data, along with illustrations and size specifications.

Once again, we can ask the question, which sheet is better? Which type of label/packing page works best for a manufacturer—an illustration type, as shown in the TechPackCentral page, or a chart type? There is no correct answer. It is up to the designer, production manager, and company owners to decide what works for them and their factories and vendors. Furthermore, the choice does not have to be either/or: the two types can be combined. There is room at the bottom of the TechPackCentral page for a chart to be added for vendor and other information. Similarly, the freelance illustrator Patrice Robson has produced pages in which label placement is sketched for the manufacturer and then dropped into a company Excel file (Box 12.1). The options for tech-pack page design are limitless.

BOX 12.1 Industry Insider Patrice Robson

The freelance apparel designer Patrice Robson works from home in Portland, Oregon, at her own design firm, Patrice Robson Design. Robson specializes in technical drawings and spec packages. Because she is an outdoor enthusiast, her designs focus on apparel for people with active lifestyles. Robson's clients have included Eddie Bauer, New Balance, and Nautilus. Prior to owning her own company, Patrice worked for Columbia Sportswear, in Portland, Oregon.

Robson's interest in design started at an early age, adjusting patterns and fabrics to make her owns clothes and learning to knit, crochet, and weave. In her twenties, Robson traveled extensively, allowing her to study the clothing and fabrics of various regions. Upon her return to the United States, Robson found work as an administrative assistant in an apparel company. At the same time, Robson attended school and was promoted to design assistant and later to designer.

Robson says, "'What we choose to wear is an individual choice and makes a statement about how we feel about ourselves and the world around us. Trends evolve with social, spiritual and economic changes. I find this one of the most fascinating aspects of design'" (Coroflot).

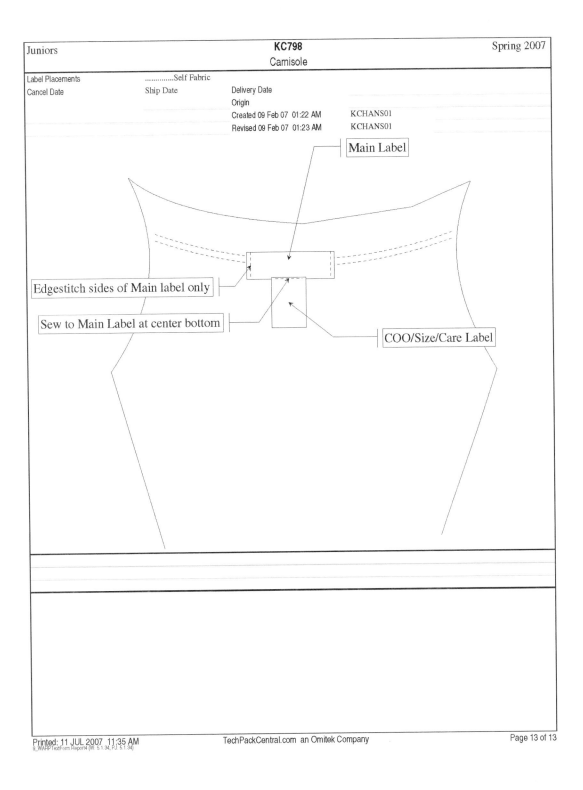

Juniors · KC798 · Camisole · Spring 2007

Label Placements ....Self Fabric
Cancel Date · Ship Date · Delivery Date
Origin
Created 09 Feb 07 01:22 AM · KCHANS01
Revised 09 Feb 07 01:23 AM · KCHANS01

Main Label

Edgestitch sides of Main label only

Sew to Main Label at center bottom

COO/Size/Care Label

Figure 12.2

(opposite) Label sheet by
TechPackCentral.

LABEL/PACKING SHEET LAB
Laboratory Applications

1. Continue the process of producing a tech-pack, this time creating a label/packing sheet. A template is provided in Figure 12.3.

2. Design you own label/packing sheet. Do you prefer the chart or illustration type? What information do you believe should be added? What should be deleted?

3. Do research on the Internet, or use trade publications, to compile a list of label and packing suppliers. How many can you find? Your instructor may assign a supplier type to each student or to groups of students for this assignment.

REFERENCE

Patrice Robson portfolio. Coroflot. http://www.coroflot.com/public/individual_details.asp?individual_id=133828 (accessed July 15, 2009).

LABEL/PACKING SHEET						PAGE #05
COMPANY NAME:			STYLE #			
ADDRESS:			GROUP NAME:			
			CLASSIFICATION:		SEASON:	
PHONE:			FABRIC CONTENT:			
FAX:			COLORWAY:			

ITEM-VENDOR-CODE-ORIGIN	CONTENT	SIZE-QUANTITY-UNIT OF MEASURE	LOCATION	COLOR	COMMENTS

DATE CREATED:	DATE MODIFIED:	DATE RELEASED:

Figure 12.3

Label/packing sheet template.

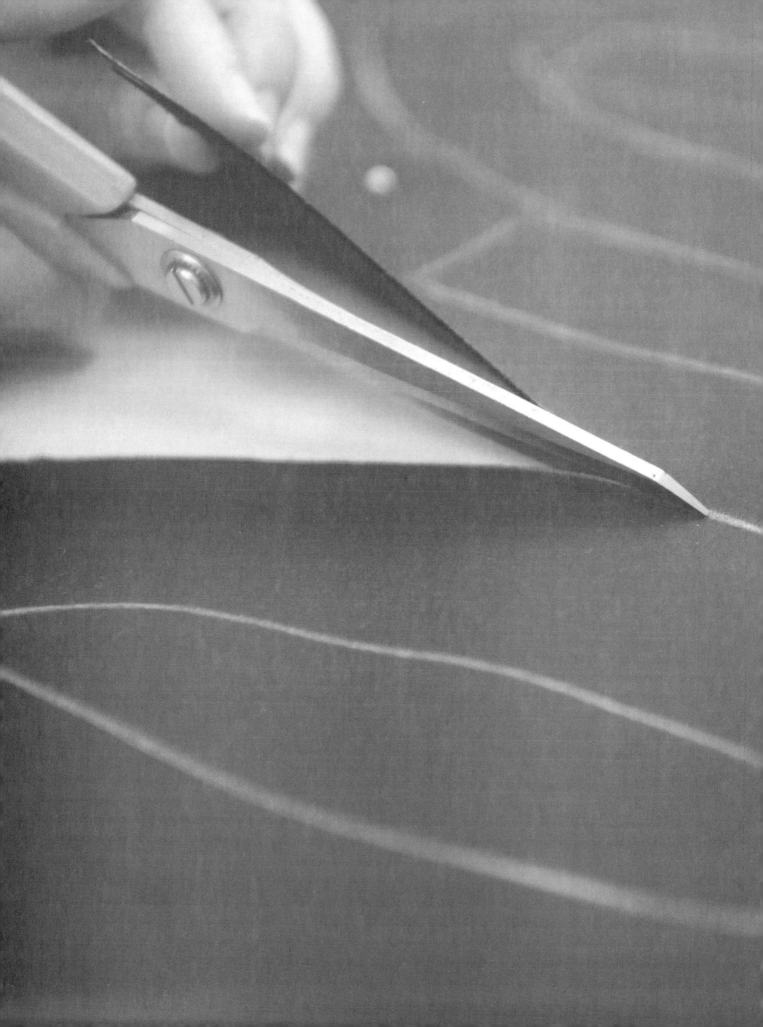

DETAIL/CONSTRUCTION SHEET: OVERVIEW

A **detail/construction sheet** lists or illustrates, or both, details (trims), and how to construct them, for production. As discussed previously, there are two distinct methods for providing this information: by illustration or by chart. This chapter's sample tech-sheet displays the illustration type, which is prevalent in industry tech-packs. Later in the chapter a chart-type sheet is also shown.

A detail/construction sheet consists of these elements:

- Company name (and occasionally its address and phone and fax numbers)
- Style or group number/name (or both)
- Season
- Fabric content
- Illustrated detail, with construction notes
- Approval boxes

HEADING   DETAIL BOXES   PAGE NUMBER

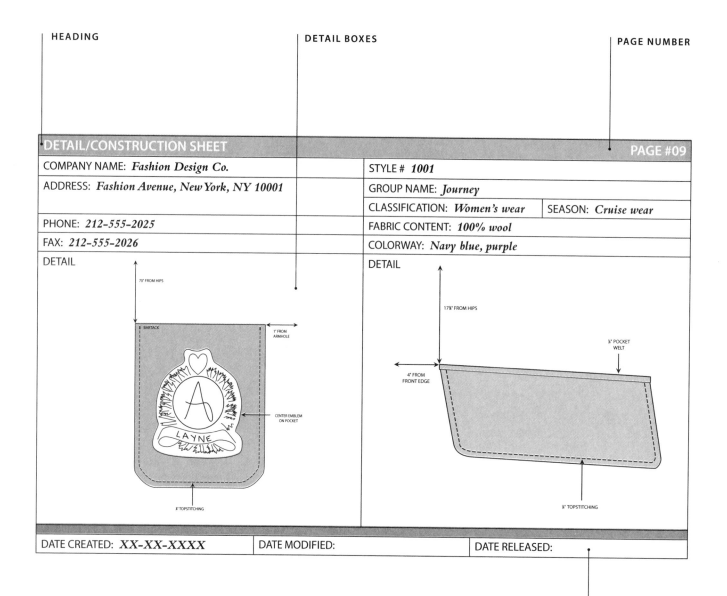

DETAIL/CONSTRUCTION SHEET   **PAGE #09**

COMPANY NAME: *Fashion Design Co.*		STYLE # *1001*	
ADDRESS: *Fashion Avenue, New York, NY 10001*		GROUP NAME: *Journey*	
		CLASSIFICATION: *Women's wear*	SEASON: *Cruise wear*
PHONE: *212-555-2025*		FABRIC CONTENT: *100% wool*	
FAX: *212-555-2026*		COLORWAY: *Navy blue, purple*	

DETAIL   DETAIL

7⅛" FROM HIPS

17⅛" FROM HIPS

BARTACK   ⅛" POCKET
                                                       WELT

1" FROM
ARMHOLE

4" FROM
FRONT EDGE

CENTER EMBLEM
ON POCKET

LAYNE

⅛" TOPSTITCHING   ⅛" TOPSTITCHING

| DATE CREATED: **XX-XX-XXXX** | DATE MODIFIED: | DATE RELEASED: |

APPROVAL BOXES

Figure 13.1

Sample detail/construction
sheet.

PREPARING A DETAIL/CONSTRUCTION SHEET

The detail/construction sheet is similar to the illustration sheet. A detailed explanation of the parts of the detail/construction sheet follows, along with instructions for preparing one. A sample sheet is provided for your reference (Figure 13.1).

HEADING
The sample shown in Figure 13.1 repeats the company name, group name, classification, basic fabric information, season, and style number.

PAGE NUMBER
The pages in the sample tech-pack continue to build; this sheet is page 9. The sheet contains only two construction details; had there been more, another page or two would have been added and the page count would have grown accordingly.

DETAIL BOXES
These boxes are for illustrating the garment trim details. The detail boxes take up most of this sheet.

APPROVAL BOXES
As always, the boxes are added to the tech-sheet to mark important production dates.

This sheet has three major sections. Because its focus is the construction details of the garment, much of the information from the other sheets is not included.

INDUSTRY DETAIL/CONSTRUCTION SHEET

Figure 13.2 is a redesign of a construction/detail sheet provided by an anonymous industry source. Although it has no illustrations, this tech-page, with its chart format, gives clear instructions for every operation or detail of construction. The sheet offers additional production information for garment construction in the seam allowance and placement sections as well. Basic information—style number, season, and so on—is at the top of the page.

As you examine these two very different tech-pack sheets, you may form an opinion as to which one you like better. Clearly, the chart type offers more information, but would there be language problems if this sheet needs to be sent to factories overseas? The illustration sheet seems clear, but does it offer enough information? Would it be better to create a sheet that combines the two approaches?

Laundry Studio creates and fits **graphic art images** to its clients' apparel designs and then uses these images for its tech-packs. The designers at Laundry need to understand illustration, construction, and design (Box 13.1).

BOX 13.1 Industry Insider Laundry Studio

Based in Portland, Oregon, Laundry Studio was founded in 2000 by Jennifer Stady and Ed Hepp. Emily Bulfin joined as a partner in 2007 after having collaborated with Laundry for many years. About their company, the partners say, "Combining our interests in art, fashion and design we provide services in creative direction, graphic design, illustration and surface design for digital, print and environmental media" (Laundry Studio). In addition to custom work for such clients as Nike, Patagonia, and Lucy, Laundry designs Laundryprints, an original textile collection that shows annually at the Indigo/Première Vision trade show in Paris. The line is sold to apparel companies, including Nau, Old Navy, and LeSportsac.

Through both its Laundryprints collection and custom work performed at the clients' direction, Laundry Studio handles construction and detail, fitting graphic images with apparel designs, and providing the images to execute tech-packs for those designs.

CONSTRUCTION SHEET	PRODUCTION: STYLE DEVELOPMENT		PAGE 4 of 8
STYLE #: *F999*	DESCRIPTION: *Jean Blazer Jacket*		STATUS:
DESIGN/PROTO #:	GROUP:		BASE SIZE: 7
DIVISION: *Juniors*	SEASON: *Fall 09*		SIZE RANGE: *00–1–3–5–7–9–11–13*
BRAND:	DESIGNER:		DATE CREATED:
PRODUCT CLASS:	PM/TECH DES.:		DATE REVISED:

OPERATION	COMMENTS
Body	*1.2" seams, pressed open, except at armhole and front facing, $^3/_8$".* *Press armhole closed. Clean finish body with lining. Clean finish sleeve to mock cuff seam.*
Hem	*Merrow and bend back 1½". Body is clean finished with lining.* *Lining ends ¾" above finished hem edge. Tack hem at all seams.*
Sleeves	*Get 2" shirring and soft gathers at sleeve cap. Center shirring between shoulder seams.*
Pockets	*Combo lining for pocket bag (same lining as sleeves), ¼" single-needle topstitch all around pocket flaps,* *backstitch flaps down at ¼" on top and bottom flap, keyhole buttonhole and button.*
Cuffs and tabs	*Mock cuff (nonadjustabel) 2¼" finished, stitched in place ¾" from cuff edge. Functional tab inserted at* *cuff seam. Tab gets ¼" topstitching all around and buttons to body. Finished tab length (buttoned) is 3".*
Buttonholes	*All buttonholes are keyhole: 4 keyhole buttonholes at CF between the welts, 2 inside buttonholes at right uperlap.* *Inside buttonholes should be at the 1st and 4th buttons. See scan page 1 of 8.*
Collar	*Collar gets single-needle ¼" topstitch at top edge and down front edge.* *Collar has a 2¼" overlap at CF, with 2 buttons and buttonholes.*
Topstitching	*¼" heavy topstitching on top collar edge and collar edge at front, CF edge, front and back princess seams,* *CB seam all around pocket flap edges, front and back empire seam and sleeve tabs.*

SEAM ALLOWANCES		PLACEMENT
Width	½"	*all other seams*
Width	$^3/_8$"	*armhole, lining armhole, front facing*
Width	¼"	*top collar edge, front welts, pocket flaps, sleeve tabs*

APPROVED BY:	
Disclaimer: Computer visuals and/or printouts of this and every sheet is for referance only. *Actual colors, patterns, and samples are provided to venders for fabrics and trims.* ***ALL PRODUCTION SAMPLES MUST BE SUBMITTED FOR APPROVAL.***	Rev. (Date):
	Rev. (Date):

Figure 13.2

Redesign of an industry detail/construction sheet (chart format).

DETAIL/CONSTRUCTION SHEET	PAGE #06

COMPANY NAME:	STYLE #
ADDRESS:	GROUP NAME:
	CLASSIFICATION: / SEASON:
PHONE:	FABRIC CONTENT:
FAX:	COLORWAY:
DETAIL	DETAIL

DATE CREATED:	DATE MODIFIED:	DATE RELEASED:

Figure 13.3

Detail/construction sheet template (illustration format).

DETAIL/CONSTRUCTION SHEET LAB
Laboratory Applications

1. Create a detail/construction sheet to add to the tech-pack you began in Chapter 7, using either an illustration (Figure 13.3) or chart (Figure 13.4) format.

2. Design your own detail/construction sheet. Do you prefer the chart or illustration type? What information do you believe should be added? What should be deleted?

3. Construction in apparel production is different from that in home sewing. Write a one- to three-page report explaining the difference. Use references to support your findings.

DETAIL/CONSTRUCTION SHEET		PAGE #06
STYLE #	DESCRIPTION:	STATUS:
DESIGN/PROTO #	GROUP:	BASE SIZE:
DIVISION:	SEASON:	SIZE RANGE:
BRAND:	DESIGNER:	DATE CREATED:
PRODUCT CLASS:	PM/TECH DES.:	DATE REVISED:

OPERATION	COMMENTS

SEAM ALLOWANCES	PLACEMENT

APPROVED BY:	
	REV. (DATE)
	REV. (DATE)

REFERENCES

Encyclopedia Britannica Online. http://www.britannica.com/#tab=active~home%2C items~home&title=Britannica%20Online%20Encyclopedia.

Laundry Studio. http://www.laundrystudio.com/ (accessed July 13, 2009).

Figure 13.4

Detail/construction sheet template (chart format).

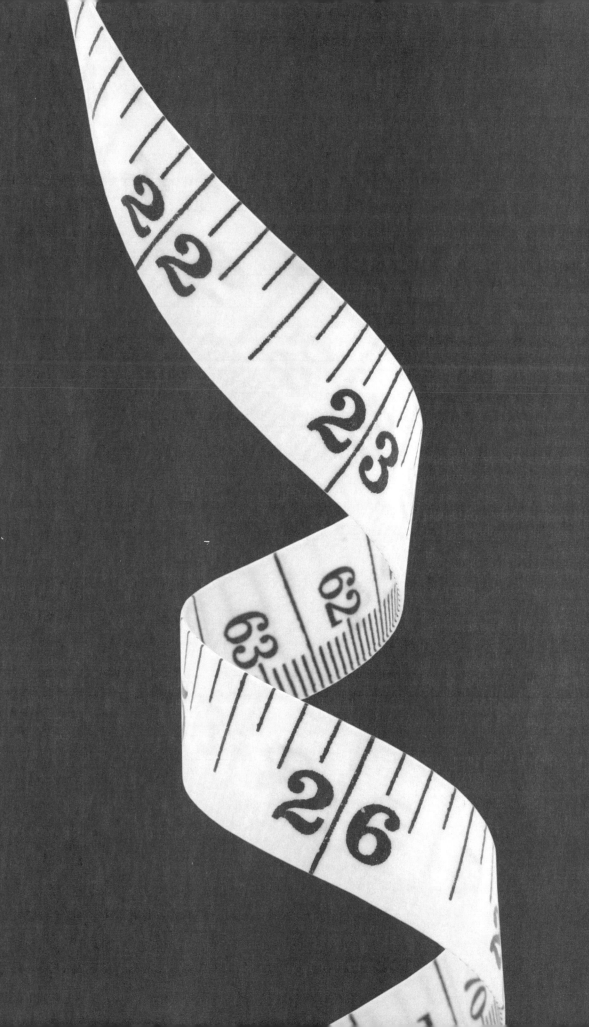

SPECIFICATION SHEET: OVERVIEW

The **specification (spec) sheet** is generally the last sheet in a tech-pack; it lists the garment measurements. Some tech-packs may include a fit session sheet. This chapter's tech-sheet is a specification sheet that provides sample measurements. Once approved for production, it would be fully graded. A fit sheet is also provided, later in the chapter.

A spec sheet is composed of the following:

- Company name (and occasionally its address and phone and fax numbers)
- Style or group number/name (or both)
- Season
- Technical sketch
- Sketch, digital illustration, or digital photo
- Measurement table
- Comments
- Approval boxes

PREPARING A SPECIFICATION SHEET

The specification sheet starts out looking like the illustration or design/component sheet; however, it is very different, as a measurement table with columns for codes, points of measure, tolerance, and sizes is included. A detailed explanation of the parts of the spec sheet follows, along with instructions for preparing one. A sample sheet is provided for your reference (Figure 14.1, next spread).

HEADING

Like all the other tech-pack sheets, this sheet has a heading: "Spec Sheet" (many industry professions use the term *spec* rather than *specification*). Again, the sample in Figure 14.1 repeats the company name, group name, classification, garment label, season, colorway, and style number. The fabric information has been eliminated because of space constraints and because a fabric sample often accompanies this sheet.

PAGE NUMBER

The text example is now up to page 10. Because two pages are needed for all the specification information, the pack ends with page 11.

GARMENT LABEL

Rather than including the fabric information, the garment label is given on this sheet. Some technicians and designers prefer to list one over the other. The choice depends on the size of the company, how many labels are involved, and so on.

MEASUREMENT TABLE

A table is the main focus of this page. At the point of production sampling, only the sample size column will be filled in; when approved for production, fully graded specs are provided. This table includes these elements:

- **Code**—The first column lists the codes given to each point of measure used. These codes correspond to numbers in the company manual. (This example uses Paula J. Myers-McDevitt's *Complete Guide to Size Specification and Technical Design* [2004].)
- **Point of measure**—The next column provides the specific points at which the garment is measured.
- **Tolerance (±)**—This column specifies the amount of acceptable measurement deviation (plus or minus) allowed during sewing.
- **Size**—The Size column lets the user know in what sizes the garment will be produced and lists the garment measurements in inches (or centimeters) for each measurement point. (Note: It is up to the manufacturer to decide whether to measure to the quarter, eighth, or sixteenth of an inch.)

COMMENTS

The Comments column lists any further information. Manufacturers may need to add additional comments pages for production corrections.

APPROVAL BOXES

Approval boxes are again added to the tech-sheet for signature dates.

This specification sheet has five sections. The measurement section is easily the focus. The technical sketch offers a quick visual and helps prevent errors that might be caused by language issues or point-of-measurement concerns. The company's spec manual should always be on hand for those working with specification sheets, to avoid confusing the measurement points.

HEADING   GARMENT LABEL   PAGE NUMBER

SPEC SHEET										PAGE #10
COMPANY NAME: *Fashion Design Co.*					STYLE #: *1001*					
ADDRESS: *Fashion Avenue, New York , NY 10001*					GROUP NAME: *Journey*					
					CLASSIFICATION: *Women's wear*			SEASON: *Cruise wear*		
PHONE: *212-555-2025*					LABEL: *A. Layne*					
FAX: *212-555-2026*					COLORWAY: *Navy Blue, purple*					

TECHNICAL SKETCH: SKETCH/PHOTO:

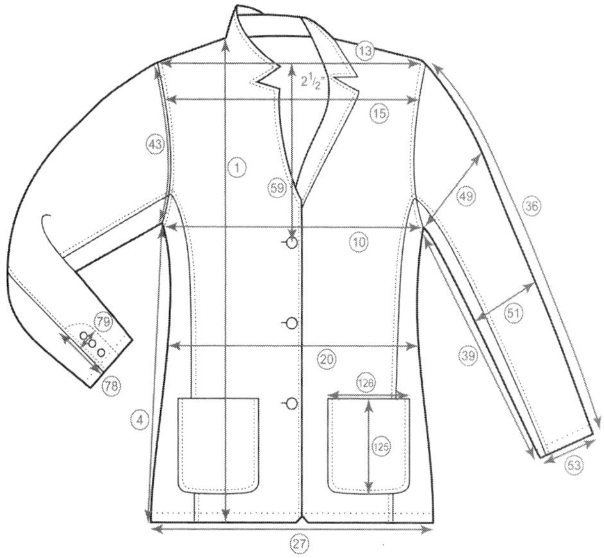

CODE		POINT OF MEASURE	TOL. ±	4 S	6	8	10 M	12	14 L	16	18 XL
1.		*Front length*	½				26				
3.		*Center back length*	½				26				
4.		*Side length*	¼				16½				
10.		*Chest width circumference*	½–¾				39				

Code   **Point of Measure**   **Tolerance**   **Size**

MEASUREMENT TABLE

Figure 14.1a

Sample specification sheet.

SPEC SHEET											PAGE #11
COMPANY NAME: *Fashion Design Co.*				STYLE #: *1001*							
CODE	**POINT OF MEASURE**	**TOL. ±**	**4**	**6 S**	**8**	**10 M**	**12**	**14 L**	**16**	**18 XL**
13.	*Across shoulder*	¼				16½				
27.	*Bottom opening/sweep width circumference*	½−¾				43				
36.	*Sleeve length top armhole*	³/₈				24¾				
39.	*Sleeve length underarm*	³/₈				17½				
43.	*Curved armhole width circumference*	³/₈				20				
49.	*Muscle width circumference*	¼				14¼				
51.	*Elbow width circumference*	¼				13¼				
53.	*Sleeve opening width circumference*	¼				10½				
59.	*Neck depth center front*	⅛				11¼				
71.	*Collar length (follow seam)*	¼				14¼				
72.	*Collar height*	⅛				2¾				
76.a	*Lapel width—notched*	⅛				3½				
78.	*Placket length (faux)*	⅛				3⁷/₈				
125.a	*Applied pocket height (chest pocket)*	⅛				5				
126.a	*Applied pocket width (chest pocket)*	⅛				4				
125.b	*Applied pocket height (pocket flaps)*	⅛				2				
126.b	*Applied pocket width (pocket flaps)*	⅛				5¼				
141.	*Shoulder pad length (along shoulder seam)*	⅛				4				
142.	*Shoulder pad width (along armhole seam)*	⅛				6				
143.	*Straight edge, shoulder pad height*	⅛				¼				
148.aa	*Pocket placement from HPC (chest pocket)*	⅛				8				
148.ab	*Pocket placement from HPS (pocket flaps)*	⅛				18¾				
150.	*Dart-length princess dart*	⅛				14³/₈				

COMMENTS: *The measurement codes and points of measure are from the text* **Complete Guide to Size Specification and Technical Design** *(Myers-McDevitt)*

DATE CREATED: *XX-XX-XXXX*	DATE MODIFIED:	DATE RELEASED:

Figure 14.1b

Sample specification sheet.

SSI BOTTOM'S SPEC SHEET							

DATE: *3/12/01*

STYLE #: *21 PFD*   STYLE NAME: *Knit Shorts*

CUSTOMER: *Style Source*

FABRIC 1: *J18 100% cotton–open end5.4osy jersey*   SHRINKAGE LxW: *8 x 3*

FABRIC 2:   SHRINKAGE LxW:

SIZE	WAIST		FR RISE		INSEAM		OUTSEAM		LEG OPENING		BK RISE					
	SPEC	3/8	SPEC	3/8	SPEC	3/4	SPEC	1	SPEC	1/4	SPEC	3/8	SPEC	SPEC	SPEC	
XS	11.250		12.833		6.180		17.614		14.272		17.357					
S	11.500		13.570		6.148		18.114		15.021		18.102					
M	12.500		14.314		6.116		18.614		15.770		18.847					
L	13.500		15.061		6.084		19.114		16.519		19.594					
XL	14.500		15.809		6.052		19.614		17.268		20.341					
2XL	15.500		16.557		6.020		20.114		18.018		21.089					

REVISIONS:

INDUSTRY SPECIFICATION SHEET

Figure 14.2 shows a very simple specification sheet produced by Style Source. We can see the company's name and, with experience, will be able to guess the season from the date and the apparel type (a pair of shorts). We know the fabric and the shrinkage factor of the fabric, which are helpful, but we have not been given a sketch of the garment or any other notations referring us to prior package pages. We can assume the garment is for a woman's division because of the sizing (XL and 2XL), and we can guess that the numbers in the size category (to the right of "Spec") are for tolerance. Finally, we can assume that because the tolerance numbers are in inches, the spec numbers are also in inches rather than centimeters, converted digitally; for example, 11.250 = 11¼. Although simple in nature, this sheet is adequate for conveying the information needed. Style Source not only manufactures its own line but also does private label (Box 14.1).

A fit measurement sheet is provided for your review in Figure 14.3 (not every tech-pack includes fit information). From this page, you can deduce that the fit garment came from the vendor based only on a designer sketch—no prior sample or specs were submitted. This is the first fit session; the design technician revised some of the measurements and corrected some construction issues. The technician noted corrections in the comments section and then asked for another sample before the start of mass production.

Figure 14.2

Style Source spec sheet.

SPECIFICATION SHEET LAB
Laboratory Applications

1. Complete your tech-pack, using the template provided (Figure 14.4, page 152) to create a specification sheet.

2. Design your own specification sheet. Do you prefer the more detailed version or the simpler one? What information do you believe should be added? What should be deleted?

3. Many catalogues and online resources offer fit charts. Check at least three, and compare your results. Are the sizes the same? If not, how do they differ? Do the company's size specifications fit your body type? What recommendations, if any, would you make to improve the charts?

REFERENCE

Myers-McDevitt, Paula J. *Complete Guide to Size Specification and Technical Design.* New York: Fairchild Publications, 2004.

BOX 14.1 Industry Insiders Heather and Geoffrey Krasnov

Style Source Inc. was founded in 2002 by a management team with over 100 years of experience in the apparel industry. Members of this team previously worked with Gee Kay Knit Products, an apparel company known for integrity, quality, and consistency.

Style Source's principals are Heather and Geoffrey Krasnov. Heather earned an MIS degree from Nichols College and possesses over 20 years of apparel experience. Prior to her work with Gee Kay Knit Products, Heather served as Product Development and Quality Manager for Crazy Shirts Hawaii.

Geoff Krasnov represents the third generation of Krasnovs in the apparel business. Geoff's grandfather founded Sure Fit Manufacturing and invented the slipcover. Geoff's father owned a number of knitting and apparel factories. A graduate of the Philadelphia College of Textiles and Science, Geoff worked in fabric development for Malden Mills, Borg Textiles, and the Sara Lee Corporation before assuming his role as Gee Kay's president in 1984. He is an active member of the American Apparel Producers Network and served as its president from 2003 to 2005.

Source: "About Style Source." Style Source Inc. http://www.geekay.com/about/index.asp (accessed July 14, 2009).

FIT MEASUREMENT SHEET — PRODUCTION SAMPLE

STYLE #: *S091426* DESCRIPTION: *Paper-bag-waist dress; solid picot with self-color topstitching*

LABEL: *Designer Collection* SIZE RANGE: *0-2-4-6-8-10-12-14-16-18* DATE CREATED: *7/17/08*

SAMPLE SIZE: *8* DATE REVISED: *9/8/08*

STATUS: MFG LOCATION: PATTERNMAKER: *Maria*

SEASON: *Spring 09* LINE PLANE PG #: *40* DESIGN TECH: *Valerie*

POM	DESCRIPTION	Tol ±	Spec	Meas 1	Var ±	Meas 2	Var ±	Revised
100	Bust 1" below armhole	½	0	38¾	38¾	0		38½
101	Waist: at seam	½	0	32¼	32¼	0		32
102	High hip: 20½" below CB pleats, closed	½	0	37½	37½	0		37½
103	Low hip: 24½" below CB pleats, closed	½	0	40	40	0		40
104	Sweep	½	0	43	43	0		43
107	Armhole	⅜	0	19¾	19¾	0		21
111	Across back shoulder	¼	0	11⅞	11⅞	0		12
112	Across back: 4" below CB	¼	0	12¼	12¼	0		12¼
113	Across front: 5" below HPS seam	¼	0	11⅞	11⅞	0		12
116	CB length: total	⅜	0	38⅜	38⅜	0		39
118	Back neck width: along edge	¼	0	8⅛	8⅛	0		8
125	Pocket opening at side seam	⅛	0	5½	5½	0		5½
128	Vent height	⅛	0	7½	7½	0		7½
136	Zipper opening	¼	0	21	21	0		22
X	Waist pleat height	⅛	0	1½	1½	0		1½

FIT COMMENTS

Corrections:

* Follow revised specs
* Waist seam should fit at natural waist
* Shape bodice waist as pinned
* Side skirt seam is going to front; adjust accordingly
* Increase pocket bag width
* Add lingerie straps

Construction:

* Be sure to topstitch with heavy topstitching thread; matching
* Follow new pattern for pocket bag width
* Use ¼" pockstitch at neck, CB, CF, princess seams, and armhole; please see Trim Sheet for correct thread color
* Use preshrunk grosgrain ribbon for lingerie straps

8/14/08 Please send revised sample for production approval

FIT SESSION: *1* DATE PRINTED: *9/17/08* TIME PRINTED: *2:24:26 PM* PAGE 4 of 4

Figure 14.3

Sample fit measurement sheet.

SPEC SHEET											PAGE #07	

COMPANY NAME:

STYLE #:

ADDRESS:

GROUP NAME:

CLASSIFICATION: | **SEASON:**

PHONE:

LABEL:

FAX:

COLORWAY:

TECHNICAL SKETCH:

SKETCH/PHOTO:

CODE	POINT OF MEASURE	TOL. ±	4 S	6	8	10 M	12	14 L	16	18 XL

COMMENTS:

DATE CREATED: | **DATE MODIFIED:** | **DATE RELEASED:**

Figure 14.4a

Spec sheet template.

SPEC SHEET										PAGE #08

COMMENTS:

DATE CREATED:	DATE MODIFIED:	DATE RELEASED:

Figure 14.4b

Spec sheet template.

Appendices

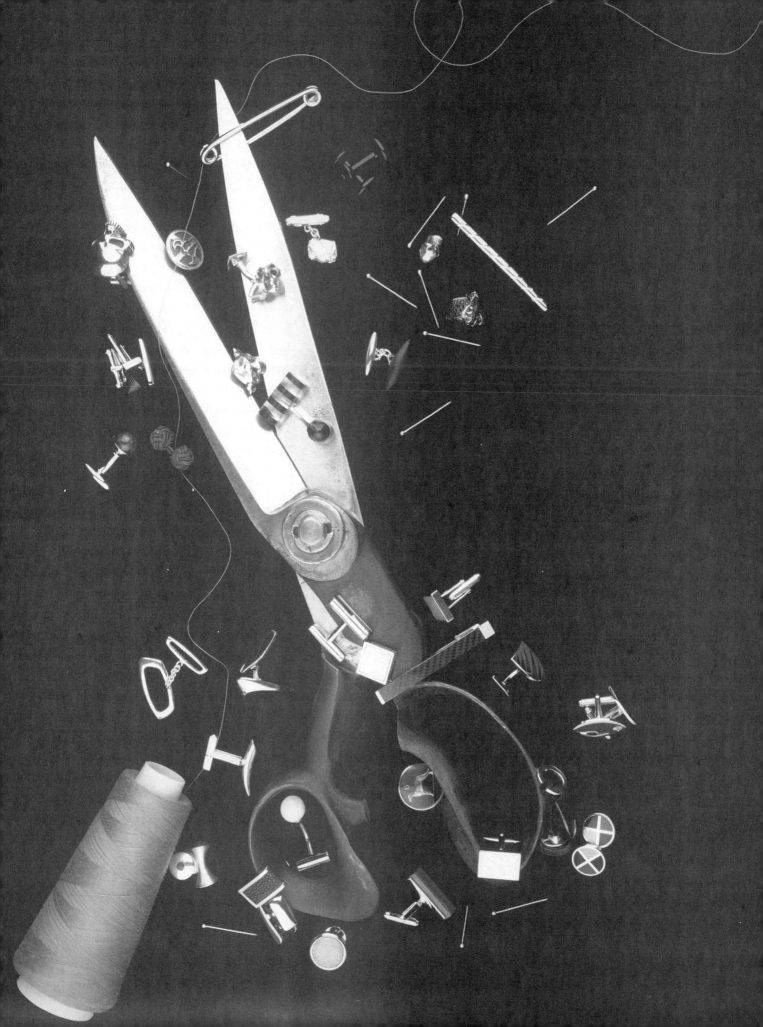

Basic Flat and Body Croquis

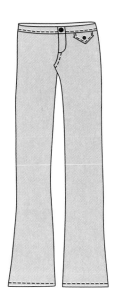

HOW TO USE FLAT-SKETCH CROQUIS

This section contains technical sketches called flats. When creating sketches for technical packages, detail is very important. Every detail, from collar to placket to pocket to button to topstitching, must be illustrated in order to ensure garment accuracy. First, garment samples may be drafted from size specifications in which the only references are the sketch and the measurements. Here are six flat sketches of the most commonly designed garments: a dress, a skirt, a pant, a jacket/blazer, a modified polo T-shirt, and a hoodie. The sketches are all uniform in (misses) proportion—size 8/10, or medium— so the user can trace or copy the garment body to be used as needed.

Flat-sketch croquis may be used as a guide for illustrating garments under evaluation. Simply trace the croquis that is closest to your garment into the "Sketch/Photo" section of your tech-pack's sheets, changing style features as needed.

The croquis may also be used to set up new specification sheets. Trace the croquis into the "Technical Sketch" section of your spec sheet. Add the appropriate measurement arrows, fill in the points of measure, and you have a custom-made spec sheet.

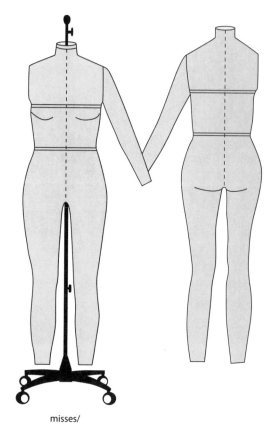

misses/
contemporary women's wear

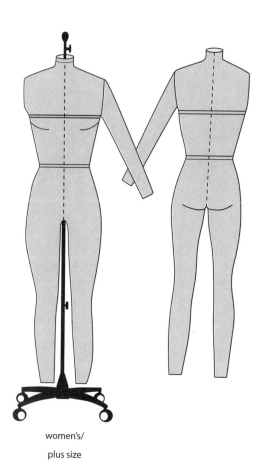

women's/
plus size

HOW TO USE BASIC BODY FORM CROQUIS

Body form croquis give a designer more freedom when sketching, although more skill is required; the designer must have the drawing skills to execute the flats, remembering to add all garment details. The end result is the same: to provide a technical sketch for the tech-pack or a spec sheet. This section contains ten body form croquis: misses/contemporary women's wear, women's/plus size, menswear, petites, juniors, girls 7 to 14, boys 8 to 20, girls/boys 4 to 6×/7, toddler (2T to 4T), and infant (12 to 24 months).

To use the body form croquis, first select the body figure that most closely matches your customer's size category. Then do your flat sketches over the body figure to give your garment scale and proportion; each body figure is drawn to scale in its size category. Finally, enter your sketch into the tech-pack as needed. Front and back views of each body size category have been provided for your convenience.

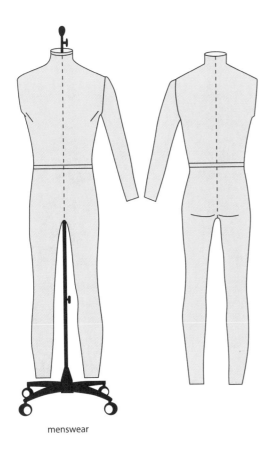

menswear

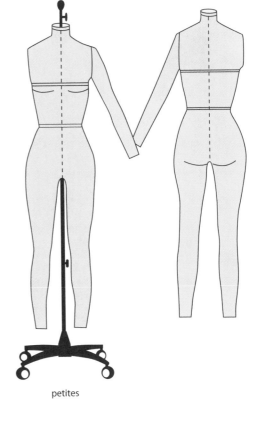

petites

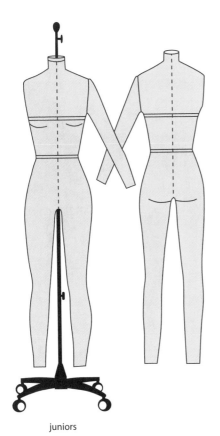

juniors

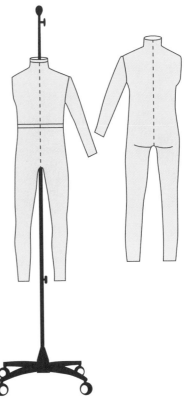

girls 7 to 14

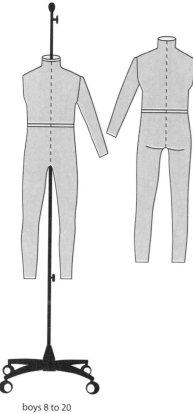

boys 8 to 20

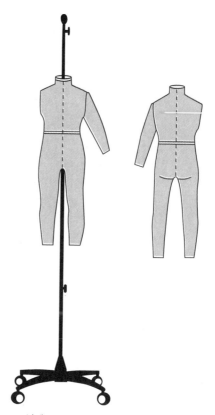

girls/boys 4 to 6x/7

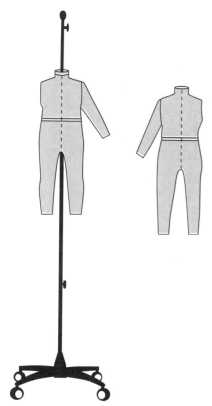

toddler (2T to 4T)

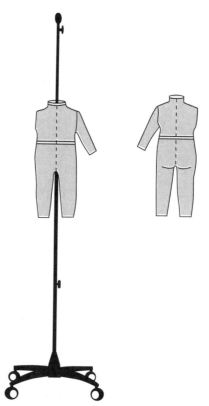

12 to 24 months

Basic Industrial Sewing Stitches

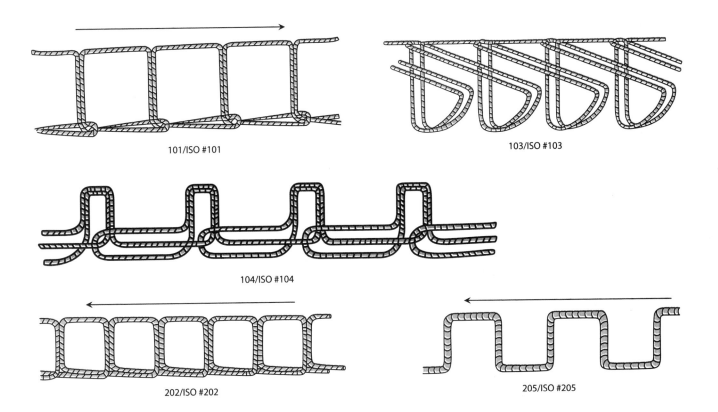

101/ISO #101

103/ISO #103

104/ISO #104

202/ISO #202

205/ISO #205

ASTM D6193-09 and ISO 4915:1991 are stitch standards that were created to allow designers, product managers, and sewing contractors ease of development and communication regarding product specification. The most common production stitch types are included here. They are broken into stitch classes 100 through 600.

ASTM International, originally known as the American Society for Testing and Materials (ASTM), was formed more than a century ago and continues to play a leadership role in addressing the standardization needs of the global marketplace ("About ASTM International"). The International Organization for Standardization (ISO) has developed more than 17,500 international standards on a variety of subjects. Some 1,100 new ISO standards are published every year ("Standards Development, International Organization for Standardization").

100-Class stitches are single-thread chain stitches using one needle thread and one blind looper. The three most widely used chain stitches are 101/ISO #101, for basting and light construction; 103/ISO #103, for blindstitch hemming; and 104/ISO #104, also for blindstitch hemming.

200-Class stitches are single-thread hand-sewn stitches using one needle thread. Two of the most widely used stitches are 202/ISO #202, for basting, tacking, and repairs, and 205, for pick stitch topstitching; there are production machines that can imitate hand pick stitching and basting.

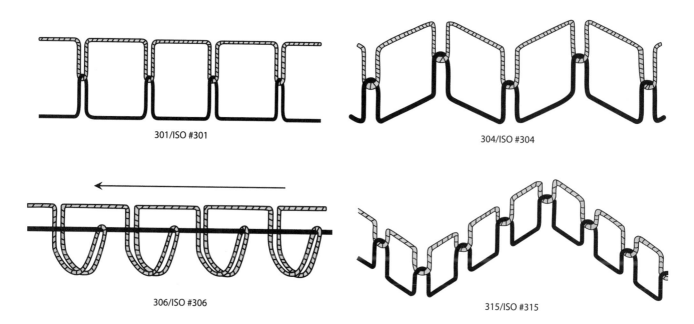

301/ISO #301

304/ISO #304

306/ISO #306

315/ISO #315

300-Class stitches are two or more thread lockstitches using the corresponding number of needles to thread and one bobbin hook thread. Of the 15 stitches in this class, the following 4 are the most frequently used: 301/ISO #301, a two-thread lockstitch that is for sewing multiple seaming plies (there is a twin–needle version of this in the ISO #301 classification that forms two rows of stitches); 304/ISO #304, a two-thread stretch zigzag lockstitch; 306/ISO #306, a two-thread blindstitch; and 315/ISO #315, a two–thread, three-step zigzag lockstitch that offers more stretch than 304.

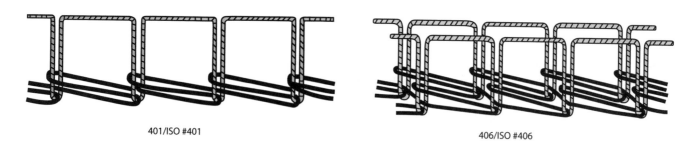

401/ISO #401

406/ISO #406

400-Class stitches are multithread chain stitches that use one or more needle threads and one or more looper threads. The two most frequently used stitches in this class are 401/ISO #401, a two-thread chain stitch that is for seaming multiple plies of fabric with moderate stretch (there is a twin needle version of this in the ISO #401 classification that forms two rows of stitches), and 406/ISO #406, a three-thread bottom cover stitch that offers a greater-stretching chain stitch.

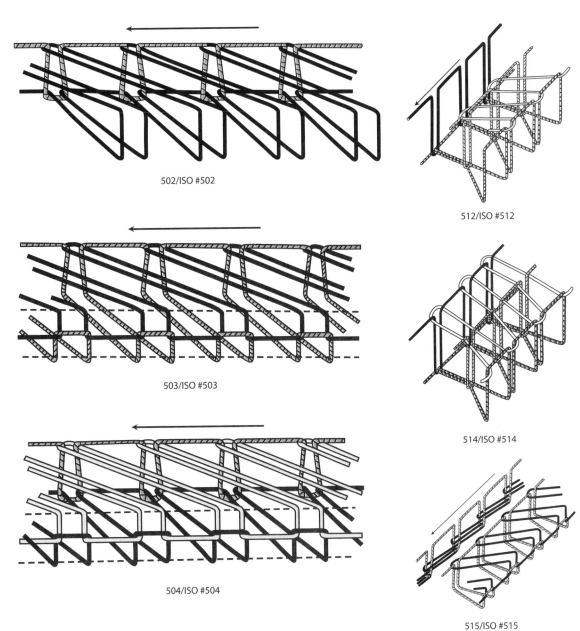

502/ISO #502

503/ISO #503

504/ISO #504

512/ISO #512

514/ISO #514

515/ISO #515

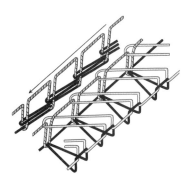

516/ISO #516

500-Class stitches are multithread over-edge chain stitches that use two or more needle threads and two or more looper threads. Of the more than 21 stitches in this class, the 7 most frequently used are 502/ISO #502, a two-thread, one-needle over-edge stitch for serging; 503/ISO #503, a two-thread over-edge stitch for serging, with a crossover on the edge of the fabric; 504/ISO #504, a three-thread over-edge serge stitch for light seaming; 512/ISO #512, a four-thread mock safety stitch for seaming, with a wide bite that offers greater stretch for knits; 514/ISO #514, a four-thread over-edge stitch also for seaming, with a wide bite that offers even greater stretch for knits; and 515/ISO #515 and 516/ISO #516, true safety stitches for seaming, offering good stretch for knits and wovens (they are four-thread and five-thread, respectively).

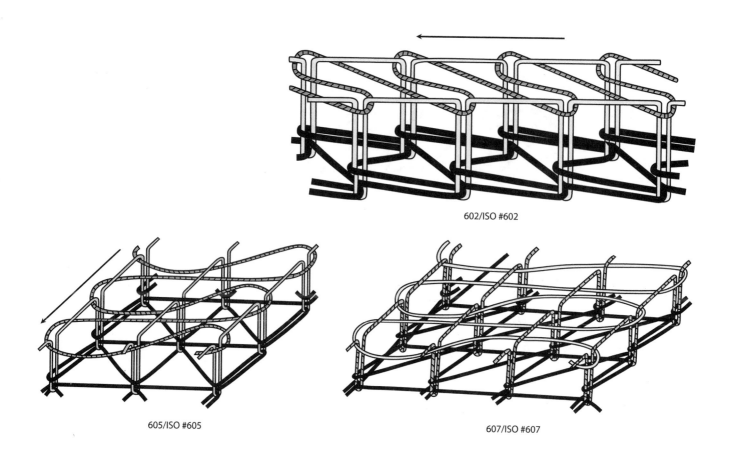

602/ISO #602

605/ISO #605

607/ISO #607

600-Class stitches are multithread cover stitches. Three stitches in this class that are widely used: 602/ISO #602 is a four-thread cover stitch for seaming knits, 605/ISO #605 is a five-thread cover stitch for "butting seams," and 607/ISO #607 is a six-thread stitch, also used for butting seams.

RESOURCES

"Stitch and Seam Guide to the ASTM Standard D-6193." Garmento.org, http://www.garmento.org/751Astitchesandseams/index.html (accessed July 18, 2009).

"Stitch Guide." Sewingcontract.com http://www.sewingcontract.com/StitchGuide.pdf (accessed July 18, 2009).

REFERENCES

"About ASTM International." ASTM International. http://www.astm.org/ABOUT/aboutASTM.html (accessed July 18, 2009).

"Standards Development." International Organization for Standardization. http://www.iso.org/iso/standards_development.htm (accessed July 18, 2009).

Button Selector Gauge

BUTTON LIGNES

Button sizes are measured in lignes. The French word *ligne,* meaning "line," was adopted in the eighteenth century by German button makers. It continues to be the internationally recognized standard today. A ligne equals $\frac{1}{40}$ inch, or 0.635 millimeters. Table A-C.1 illustrates popular button sizes measured in millimeters and converted to lignes. This chart can be used to measure a button or decide the size of a prospective button (Table A-C.1).

TABLE A-C.1 **Ligne to Inch Conversion Table**

LIGNES	18	20	22	24	28	30	32	34	36	40
METRIC	12	13	14	15	17	19	20	21	23	25
INCHES	$3/8"$	$1/2"$	$9/16"$	$5/8"$	$11/16"$	$3/4"$	$5/6"$	$6/7"$	$7/8"$	$1"$

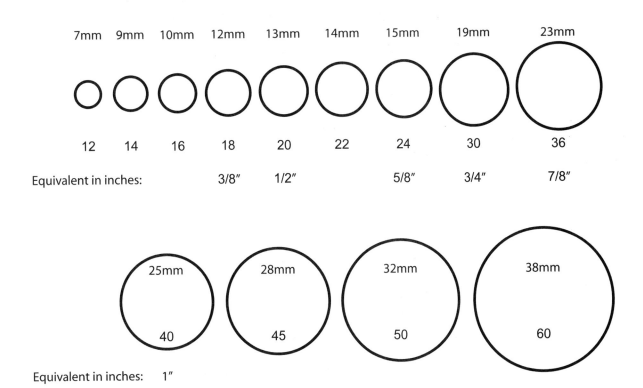

TABLE A-C.2   **Button Size and Buttonhole Length Chart**

BUTTON SIZE (DIAMETER MEASURED IN LIGNES)			BUTTONHOLE LENGTH	BUTTONHOLE LENGTH
LIGNES	MILLIMETERS	INCHES	MILLIMETERS	INCHES
12	7.5	$5/16$"	9.0–9.4 mm	$11/32$"–$3/8$"
14	9.2	$3/8$"	11.1–11.5 mm	$7/16$"–$15/32$"
15	10.0	$13/32$"	12.0–12.5 mm	$15/32$"–$1/2$"
16	10.5	$5/8$"	12.6–13.1 mm	$1/2$"–$17/32$"
18	11.6	$7/16$"	13.9–14.5 mm	$17/32$"–$9/16$"
19	12.0	$15/32$"	14.4–15.0 mm	$9/16$"–$19/32$"
20	12.7	$1/2$"	15.2–15.9 mm	$19/32$"–$5/8$"
22	14.2	$9/16$"	17.0–17.8 mm	$21/32$"–$11/16$"
24	15.1	$19/32$"	18.2–18.9 mm	$23/32$"–$3/4$"
27	17.0	$21/32$"	20.4–21.3 mm	$13/16$"–$27/32$"
28	17.8	$11/16$"	21.4–22.3 mm	$27/32$"–$7/8$"
30	19.1	$3/4$"	22.9–23.9 mm	$29/32$"–$15/16$"
32	20.5	$13/16$"	24.2–25.3 mm	$31/32$"–1"
34	21.5	$27/32$"	25.8–26.9 mm	1"–1 $1/32$"
36	23.0	$29/32$"	27.6–28.8 mm	1 $1/16$"–1 $3/32$"
40	25.5	1"	30.6–31.9 mm	1 $3/32$"–1 $1/8$"

BUTTONHOLES

Buttonholes should be approximately 20 to 25 percent longer than the length of the button. If a fusible or canvas-type interlining has been applied to the hole, the dimension can be lowered to as little as 15 percent. A smaller measurement is also recommended for very lightweight fabrics (Table A-C.2).

When buttonholes are too small for the coordinating buttons, button-sew failure may arise. Generally, such failure is due to the unraveling of buttonhole stitches, but when buttonholes are not sewn to proportion, strain is created on the threads, causing them to break. To provide a stronger buttonhole, and thus prevent both unraveling and breakage, a lockstitch buttonhole machine (rather than a chain-stitch buttonhole machine) should be used.

REFERENCES

Bryant, Michele Wesen, and Diane DeMers. *The Spec Manual.* 2nd ed. New York: Fairchild Publications, 2006.

"Thread Recommendations for Buttonsewing, Buttonholes, and Bartacks." American and Efird. http://www.amefird.com/buttonhole.htm (accessed May 27, 2009).

Care Labeling Regulations

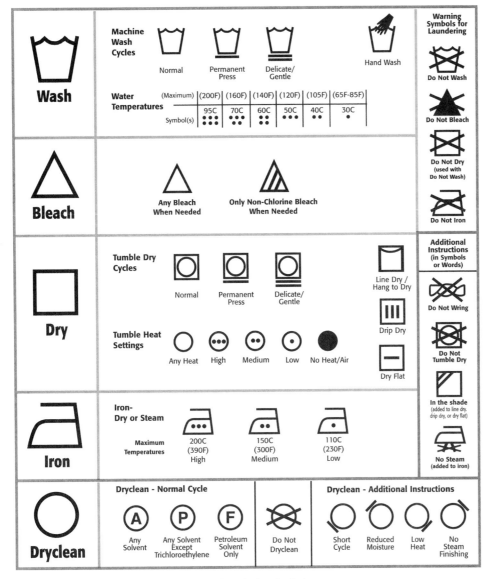

Apparel/Textile Care Symbols

Apparel manufacturers must follow federal and state regulations for the labeling and marketing of fibers, yarns, and other textile products sold in the United States. In 1971, the Federal Trade Commission passed a set of rules on care labeling—"Care Labeling of Textile Wearing Apparel and Certain Piece Goods." These regulations (which were amended in 1983) were designed to protect the rights of the consumer to know how properly to care for garments before and after purchase.

The rules require that a permanent label with care instructions be attached to a garment; the instructions may be made up of text or care symbols, or a combination of these.

REFERENCE

Nadiger, G. S. "Care Labeling of Textile Apparels." *Journal of the Textile Association* 68, no. 1: 7–18. http://www.textileassociationindia.org/JTA_ISSUES/Page%20 No.%207%20to%2018.pdf (accessed July 15, 2009).

Size Specification: Basic Measurement Points

HOW TO USE BASIC MEASUREMENT POINTS

This section contains basic measurement points used on a specification sheet. When you are creating a spec sheet, detail is very important. Every detail, from the length and width of the garment, pockets, waistband in pants, collars in blouses or jackets, and sleeves, must be measured in order to ensure garment accuracy. First, garment samples may be drafted from size specifications in which the only references are the sketch and the measurements. This section contains over 153 measurement points. It is up to the spec technician to decide which ones need to be used for the garment being measured.

1. Front length (garments with a front opening)
2. Center-front length (garments with a plain front, no front opening)
3. Center-back length
4. Side length
5. Front bodice length (garments with a front opening)
6. Center-front bodice length (garments with a plain front, no front opening)
7. Center-back bodice length
8. Side seam bodice length
9. Chest width (knit)
10. Chest width circumference (woven)
11. Chest width (raglan sleeve, knit)
12. Chest width circumference (raglan sleeve, woven)
13. Across shoulder
14. Shoulder width
15. Across chest
16. Across back
17. Across chest, center armhole
18. Across back, center armhole
19. Waist width (knit)
20. Waist width circumference (woven)
21. Bottom band width (knit top)
22. Bottom band circumference (woven top)
23. Bottom band width, stretched (knit top)

24. Bottom band width circumference, stretched (woven top)
25. Bottom band/ribbing height (knit or woven top)
26. Bottom opening/sweep (knit top)
27. Bottom opening/sweep width circumference (woven top)
28. Vented bottom opening/sweep width (knit top)
29. Vented bottom opening/sweep width circumference (woven top)
30. Circular bottom opening/sweep width (knit top)
31. Circular bottom opening/sweep width circumference (woven top)
32. Yoke width, front
33. Yoke width, back
34. Yoke depth, front
35. Yoke depth, back
36. Sleeve length, top armhole
37. Sleeve length, top neck
38. Sleeve length, center back
39. Sleeve length, underarm
40. Straight armhole width (knit)
41. Straight armhole width circumference (woven)
42. Curved armhole width (knit)
43. Curved armhole width circumference (woven)
44. Armhole, front
45. Armhole, back
46. Armhole width straight (knit)
47. Armhole width circumference straight (woven)
48. Muscle width (knit)
49. Muscle width circumference (woven)
50. Elbow width (knit)
51. Elbow width circumference (woven)
52. Sleeve opening width (knit)
53. Sleeve opening width circumference (woven)
54. Sleeve opening width, stretched (knit)
55. Sleeve opening width circumference, stretched (woven)
56. Cuff length, sleeve
57. Cuff/ribbing height, sleeve
58. Neck depth, front (garments with a plain front/asymmetrical front opening)
59. Neck depth, center front (garments with a center front opening)
60. Neck drop, front
61. Neck drop, back
62. Neck width, no collar
63. Neck width, collar
64. Neck edge width (knit)
65. Neck edge width circumference (woven)

66. Neck edge width, stretched (knit)
67. Neck edge width circumference, stretched (woven)
68. Neck base (knit)
69. Neck base circumference (woven)
70. Neckband length
71. Collar length
72. Collar height
73. Collar band height
74. Collar point length
75. Collar point spread (pointed collars only)
76. Lapel width
    a. Notched
    b. Without notches
77. Center front extension
78. Placket length
79. Placket width
80. Keyhole length
81. Waistband depth
82. Waistband width (knit)
83. Waistband circumference (woven)
84. Waistband width, stretched (knit)
85. Waistband width circumference, stretched (woven)
86. High hip width (knit)
87. High hip width circumference (woven)
88. Low hip width from waist (knit)
89. Low hip width circumference from waist (woven)
90. Hip width from HPS (knit)
91. Hip width from HPS circumference (woven)
92. Hip seat width (knit pant)
93. Hip seat width circumference (woven pant)
94. Bottom opening/sweep width (knit skirt)
95. Bottom opening/sweep width circumference (woven skirt)
96. Vented bottom opening/sweep width (knit skirt)
97. Vented bottom opening/sweep width circumference (woven skirt)
98. Circular bottom opening/sweep width (knit skirt)
99. Circular bottom opening/sweep width circumference (woven skirt)
100. Center-front skirt length
101. Center-back skirt length
102. Side skirt length
103. Skirt/pant yoke depth, front
104. Skirt/pant yoke depth, back
105. Inseam

106. Outseam

107. Front rise

108. Back rise

109. Thigh width (knit)

110. Thigh width circumference (woven)

111. Knee width (knit)

112. Knee width circumference (woven)

113. Leg opening width (knit)

114. Leg opening width circumference (woven)

115. Vented leg opening width (knit)

116. Vented leg opening circumference (woven)

117. Leg opening width, stretched (knit)

118. Leg opening width circumference, stretched (woven)

119. Cuff height, pants

120. Bottom band/ribbing height, pants

121. Fly/zipper

    a. Length

    b. Fly/zipper width

122. Vent/slit

    a. Height

    b. Width

123. Pleat depth

124. Distance between pleats

125. Applied pocket height

126. Applied pocket width

127. Pocket opening within a seam

128. Belt length

    a. Total

    b. Circumference

129. Belt width (or height)

130. Belt loop length

131. Belt loop width

132. Tie length

133. Tie width

    a. Straight

    b. Contoured

134. Flounce/ruffle width

135. Strap length

136. Strap width

137. Front hood length

138. Back hood length

139. Hood width

140. Flange depth

141. Shoulder pad length

142. Shoulder pad width

143. Straight-edge shoulder pad height

144. Curved-edge shoulder pad height

145. Shoulder pad placement

146. Pleats placement

    a. Front pleat, top

    b. Back pleat, top

    c. Front pleat, skirt/pant

    d. Back pleat, skirt

147. Button placement

148. Pocket placement

    a. Top pocket vertical

    b. Top pocket horizontal

    c. Front bottom pocket vertical

    d. Front bottom pocket horizontal

    e. Back bottom pocket vertical

    f. Back bottom pocket horizontal

    g. Pocket from side seam

149. Belt loop placement

    a. Front

    b. Back

    c. Side seam to front

    d. Side seam to back

150. Dart placement

    a. High point shoulder bust dart

    b. Center-front bust dart

    c. Side seam bust dart

    d. High point shoulder princess dart

    e. Center-front princess dart

    f. Center-front skirt/pant

    g. Center-back skirt/pant

151. Front torso length (jumpsuits and one-piece garments)

    a. Garments with a front opening relaxed

    b. Garments with a front opening extended

    c. Garments with a plain front, no front opening, relaxed

    d. Garments with a plain front, no front opening, extended

152. Back torso length (jumpsuits and one-piece garments)

    a. Relaxed

    b. Extended

153. High point shoulder length (jumpsuits and one-piece garments)

REFERENCE

Myers-McDevitt, Paula J. *Complete Guide to Size Specification and Technical Design.* New York: Fairchild Publications, 2004.

Tech-Pack Templates

DESIGN SHEET	PAGE #01

COMPANY NAME:	STYLE #
ADDRESS:	SKETCH
PHONE:	
FAX:	

GARMENT INFORMATION

GROUP NAME:
CLASSIFICATION:
SEASON:
GARMENT LABEL:
FABRIC CONTENT:
COLORWAY:
DESCRIPTION:

Designer Initials

DATE CREATED:	DATE MODIFIED:	DATE RELEASED:

ILLUSTRATION SHEET		PAGE #02
COMPANY NAME:	STYLE #	
ADDRESS:	GROUP NAME:	
	CLASSIFICATION:	SEASON:
PHONE:	GARMENT LABEL:	
FAX:	COLORWAY:	

SKETCH

Designer Initials

FABRIC INFORMATION	STYLE WIDTH	SIZE RANGES	DELIVERY DATE	COMMENTS

DATE CREATED:	DATE MODIFIED:	DATE RELEASED:

FABRIC SHEET		PAGE #03

COMPANY NAME:	STYLE #	
ADDRESS:	GROUP NAME:	
	CLASSIFICATION:	SEASON:
PHONE:	GARMENT LABEL:	
FAX:	COLORWAY:	

SKETCH	SWATCH

Designer Initials

FABRIC INFORMATION	STYLE WIDTH	SIZE RANGES	DELIVERY DATE	COMMENTS

DATE CREATED:	DATE MODIFIED:	DATE RELEASED:

COMPONENT SHEET						PAGE #04
COMPANY NAME:			STYLE #			
ADDRESS:			GROUP NAME:			
			CLASSIFICATION:		SEASON:	
PHONE:			FABRIC CONTENT:			
FAX:			COLORWAY:			

ITEM-VENDOR-CODE-ORIGIN	CONTENT	SIZE-QUANTITY-UNIT OF MEASURE	LOCATION	COLOR	COMMENTS

DATE CREATED:	DATE MODIFIED:	DATE RELEASED:

LABEL/PACKING SHEET						PAGE #05
COMPANY NAME:			STYLE #			
ADDRESS:			GROUP NAME:			
			CLASSIFICATION:		SEASON:	
PHONE:			FABRIC CONTENT:			
FAX:			COLORWAY:			
ITEM-VENDOR-CODE-ORIGIN	CONTENT	SIZE-QUANTITY-UNIT OF MEASURE		LOCATION	COLOR	COMMENTS
DATE CREATED:		DATE MODIFIED:			DATE RELEASED:	

DETAIL/CONSTRUCTION SHEET		PAGE #06
COMPANY NAME:	STYLE #	
ADDRESS:	GROUP NAME:	
	CLASSIFICATION:	SEASON:
PHONE:	FABRIC CONTENT:	
FAX:	COLORWAY:	
DETAIL	DETAIL	

DATE CREATED:	DATE MODIFIED:	DATE RELEASED:

DETAIL/CONSTRUCTION SHEET		PAGE #06
STYLE #	DESCRIPTION:	STATUS:
DESIGN/PROTO #	GROUP:	BASE SIZE:
DIVISION:	SEASON:	SIZE RANGE:
BRAND:	DESIGNER:	DATE CREATED:
PRODUCT CLASS:	PM/TECH DES.:	DATE REVISED:

OPERATION	COMMENTS

SEAM ALLOWANCES	PLACEMENT

APPROVED BY:	
	REV. (DATE)
	REV. (DATE)

SPEC SHEET										PAGE #07

COMPANY NAME:

STYLE #:

ADDRESS:

GROUP NAME:

CLASSIFICATION: **SEASON:**

PHONE:

LABEL:

FAX:

COLORWAY:

TECHNICAL SKETCH:

SKETCH/PHOTO:

CODE	POINT OF MEASURE	TOL. ±	4 S	6	8	10 M	12	14 L	16	18 XL

COMMENTS:

DATE CREATED: **DATE MODIFIED:** **DATE RELEASED:**

SPEC SHEET											PAGE #08

COMMENTS:

DATE CREATED: | DATE MODIFIED: | DATE RELEASED:

Glossary

Adobe Illustrator A computer-based drawing tool created by Adobe Systems.

Assembly The fitting together of smaller parts (components) into a complete structure, or unit.

Bar code A computer code represented by a pattern of bars that can be read by a laser scanner and that is used to identify merchandise.

Codes The numbering (or lettering) system given to the measurement points.

Colorway A set of colors.

Component sheet A sheet that lists every component or constituent part of the garment.

Cost The total dollar value given in expenditures, time, and energy, required to receive services and produce goods.

Costing method The procedure a company utilizes to track all expenses and income coming in and going out.

Detail/Construction sheet A tech-sheet that lists or illustrates, or both, details (trims) and how to construct them for production.

Design sheet The first sheet of a technical package.

Digital illustration Computer-generated bitmap or vector art using digital tools manipulated by the artist, generally with a mouse or graphics tablet/screen.

Digital photo An image captured on a digital camera or scanner and converted into an array of binary numbers (bitmap file) that a computer can process. Tagged Image File Format (TIFF) is one popular image data format used.

Distribution The delivery of merchandise from handling facilities.

Fabric A cloth of any type made from woven, knitted, or felted thread or fibers.

Fabric sheet A technical package sheet that shows a swatch or digital image of the fabric and that lists the fabric information.

Finishing The process or processes that give the garment its final appearance.

Graphic art image A visual representation combining images and symbols to convey a message that can be produced by hand drawing or computer-aided design (CAD), or a combination of these.

Hangtag A merchandise tag that provides information about the item's manufacturer and composition as well as proper care and use; bar codes are included.

Garment component Identifiable part or piece that is required for assembly of a garment.

Hangtag A decorative tag attached to an article of merchandise that provides information about its size and cost.

Illustration sheet The sheet in a technical package that shows the various colorways of a garment or detailed front and back views, or both.

Label A slip of cloth inscribed and affixed to a garment for identification or description that shows the brand name of the retail store, the clothing manufacturer, or the fashion designer, as well as care information and garment size.

Label/Packing sheet A sheet that lists all the data used to label or package (or both) a garment.

Labor In apparel production, the collection of all human physical and mental effort used in creation of goods.

Long-term planning A means of meeting future needs and predicting future data by using charts and plans reflecting present status and then projecting a path for achieving interim goals.

Materials handling The entire process of garment assembly.

Microsoft Excel A spreadsheet application that can be used on both Microsoft Windows and Macintosh operating systems.

Packaging Presenting a product in such a way as to heighten its appeal to the public; for example, using hangtags, protective plastic, or a box.

Point of measure A specific point at which a garment is measured.

Preproduction planning The process of coordinating the premanufacturing operations to be performed by different functions and workstations over a particular time period.

Production capabilities Measure of the ability or output of the plant (machine work center, work center, person, system) to achieve its objectives, especially in relation to its overall mission, in a given period of time.

Product cost The sum of all costs associated with the production of a specific quantity of goods.

Product Data Management (PDM) A business function within the Product Lifecycle Management system that allows for the creation and tracking of product management data.

Production department A department within a company in which people work who are responsible for manufacturing goods in large quantities.

Production manager The manager of the employees who work in the production department. One of the tools the production manager uses to ensure smooth execution is the technical package, also known as the tech-pack.

Production planning The process of coordinating the manufacturing operations to be performed by different functions and workstations over a particular period.

Production samples Garments made for evaluation, selected to represent the characteristics of the entire group, establishing a standard for quality, cost, and performance. It is implied that production will conform to this standard; otherwise, the producer or supplier may be held liable.

Production team The employees who work in the production department. Coordination of tasks and precision are necessary in order for a team to work together successfully

Product Lifecycle Management (PLM) A system that manages the entire life cycle of the product: conception, design, manufacture, service, and disposal.

Profit The surplus remaining after total costs are deducted from total revenue; also known as earning, gain, or income.

Quick Response Delivery System (QR) A business strategy designed to reduce the lead time for receiving merchandise, thereby reducing the amount of inventory on hand, decreasing distribution expenses, and allowing for quicker reorders, thus enhancing customer service levels.

Quick Response Manufacturing System A system designed to reduce the lead time in every step of the manufacturing process.

Scheduling The process of assigning start and completion times to manufacturing based on availability of plant and materials, customer delivery requirements, and maintenance schedules.

Short-term planning In general, a plan with a business focus of five years or less; also called *short-range planning*.

Sourcing agent A person whose main goal is to work with both the buyer and the manufacturer to produce items according to their quality and engineering specifications.

Specification (spec) sheet A standardized list of garment measurements consisting of style information, technical renderings, points of measure, size ranges, and garment measurements.

Style assignment Choosing a manufacturer-owned or contracted plant to produce goods as soon as they have been adopted into the line and production is estimated.

Technical package An assemblage of informative sheets encompassing all required garment specifications that is collected before embarking on garment manufacturing.

Tolerance The amount of acceptable measurement deviation (plus or minus) allowed during sewing.

U.S. labeling laws Requirement by the U.S. government to attach to an apparel item for sale label(s) containing information about that garment (see Appendix D).

Credits

Part I Opener Image: Courtesy of Veer
Chapter 1 Opener Image: Courtesy of Veer
Chapter 2 Opener Image: © David Selman/Corbis
Chapter 3 Opener Image: Courtesy of iStockphoto
Part II Opener Image: © Manchan/Getty Images
Chapter 4 Opener Image: © Image Source/Corbis
Chapter 5 Opener Image: Courtesy of iStockphoto
Chapter 6 Opener Image: Courtesy of iStockphoto
Part III Opener Image: Courtesy of iStockphoto
Chapter 7 Opener Image: Courtesy of Veer
Chapter 8 Opener Image: Courtesy of iStockphoto
Chapter 9 Opener Image: Courtesy of iStockphoto
Chapter 10 Opener Image: Courtesy of Fotosearch
Chapter 11 Opener Image: Courtesy of Veer
Chapter 12 Opener Image: Courtesy of iStockphoto
Chapter 13 Opener Image: © Picture Contact/Alamy
Chapter 14 Opener Image: Courtesy of iStockphoto
Appendix Part Opener Image: Courtesy of iStockphoto
Appendix Chapter Opener Image: Courtesy of Veer

Index